INNOVATIVE MINDS

LEWIS LATIMER
CREATING BRIGHT IDEAS

Eleanor Ayer

RSVP

RAINTREE STECK-VAUGHN
PUBLISHERS
The Steck-Vaughn Company

Austin, Texas

Published by Raintree Steck-Vaughn Publishers, an imprint of Steck-Vaughn Company.

Series created by Blackbirch Graphics
Series Editor: Tanya Lee Stone
Editor: Lisa Clyde Nielsen
Associate Editor: Elizabeth M. Taylor
Production/Design Editor: Calico Harington

Raintree Steck-Vaughn Staff
Editors: Shirley Shalit, Kathy DeVico
Project Manager: Lyda Guz

Library of Congress Cataloging-in-Publication Data

Ayer, Eleanor H.
    Lewis Latimer : creating bright ideas / by Eleanor Ayer.
        p.   cm. — (Innovative minds)
    Includes bibliographical references and index.
    Summary: A biography of the self-educated son of former slaves, describing the positive outlook and determination that allowed him to overcome poverty and racism and become a successful inventor.
    ISBN 0-8172-4407-7
    1. Latimer, Lewis, 1848–1928—Juvenile literature. 2. Afro-American inventors—Biography—Juvenile literature. [1. Latimer, Lewis Howard, 1848–1928. 2. Inventors. 3. Afro-Americans—Biography.]   I. Title. II. Series.
T40.L37A94   1997
609'.2—dc20
[B]
                                        96-18930
                                            CIP
                                            AC

Printed in the United States of America
1 2 3 4 5 6 7 8 9 0 LB 00 99 98 97 96

Table of Contents

Lewis Latimer made great contributions to the field of electric lighting.

THE SON OF
FUGITIVE
SLAVES

The year was 1878, and the place was Menlo Park, New Jersey—home of the famous inventor Thomas Alva Edison. At that time, people in Menlo Park, like those in other American cities and towns, lighted their homes with lamps that burned kerosene or natural gas delivered to houses through pipes. But the burning of these fuels blackened walls and ceilings, and they could be dangerous. Without careful handling, they could burn out of control, or even explode. Many people who used natural gas and kerosene suffered from dizziness or headaches because of the fumes produced as the fuels burned. And if any gas leaked as it was transported through the pipes, the ground and water became contaminated.

Outside, the streets were lit with gas lamps. Arc lighting, a type of electric light, was also being used. But arc lighting had many drawbacks. The lights were noisy, emitting a hissing sound, and they threw off sparks. They were extremely bright—not the sort of soft light that many people liked. A better lighting system was needed.

In his Menlo Park laboratory, Thomas Edison was working on this problem. Ever since he had taken a trip to the Rocky Mountains and seen miners drilling laboriously into the hard rock with hand-operated tools, Edison had wanted to use electricity to bring power and light to businesses and homes. He was convinced that it was possible and that he would be the one to achieve it.

In Search of a Better Bulb

Edison, like other inventors of his time, had done laboratory experiments to develop bulbs that would provide good lighting. They had discovered that a thin, flexible strand called a filament, heated inside a vacuum—a sealed space where no air or other matter exists—would glow to produce light. A copper wire that ran from a power source to the filament would carry the electricity that allowed the filament to burn.

But there was one big problem: Neither Edison nor other inventors had found the right material for the filament. For months, Edison had been using platinum, a silver-white metallic element. He did many experiments with platinum, but over time it proved unworkable. It was much too expensive, and Edison found that it didn't burn long enough to be suitable for a lightbulb.

The famous inventor Thomas Edison was among those scientists looking for the best material from which to make lightbulb filaments.

Edison had experimented earlier with carbonized paper—paper that has been reduced to carbon by burning under the proper conditions. He tried to use it as a material for filaments, and when platinum proved unworkable, he returned to that idea. He had discovered that cellulose, one of the substances in paper, burned well inside the vacuum. As it burned, it turned the paper into a thin frame of carbon. The electric current that traveled along the copper wire into the filament kept the carbonized paper frame glowing for quite some time.

Edison knew that there were materials other than paper that could be carbonized, and he suspected that one of these might burn longer and better. Other inventors had experimented with different materials, among them common cotton sewing thread. Edison decided to perform a new set of experiments with thread, and the results of these experiments made history. In the early morning hours of October 22, 1879, reported *The New York Herald* newspaper, the carbonized thread filament produced what the newspaper described as "a little globe of sunshine, a veritable Aladdin's lamp" that glowed with the light of 30 candles.

In his journal, Edison wrote about the magic of that night, describing his fascination as the lamp burned on and on. The bulb actually burned for 45 hours. Thrilled with the results, Edison filed for a legal patent on November 1, 1879. A patent would ensure that no other inventors could copy Edison's idea and claim it as their own.

Excited as he was with his success, however, he was not entirely satisfied with the carbonized thread filament. Along with dozens of other inventors around the world, he continued experimenting with different substances to find the proper filament. He tried fishing line, hair, wood chips, coconut shell—but none of these materials produced a cheaper, longer-lasting filament.

Among the other inventors who were working to solve the filament problem was Lewis Latimer. This soft-spoken young man from Boston, Massachusetts, had recently gone to work for Hiram Maxim, one of Edison's chief rivals in the development of electric lighting. Latimer was a patient and methodical person. A self-taught draftsman, or drafter —a person who makes technical drawings and plans—he had a great deal of experience in writing and illustrating applications for patents.

But Latimer also developed ideas of his own. He had learned a great deal about electricity in the short time he had worked for Maxim's U.S. Electric Lighting Company. Now he put his knowledge to work to find a long-lasting and inexpensive filament for lightbulbs.

For many months after Edison's initial success, Latimer labored over the problem of a better filament. He performed hundreds of experiments with various carbonized materials, convinced that one of them would unlock the filament mystery. At last, in 1881, Latimer discovered the system for which he had been searching. He created his filament by inserting small pieces of wood or paper into tiny cardboard envelopes and burning them at very high temperatures. Placing the material inside the envelopes allowed it to burn longer. To prevent the pieces of wood or paper from sticking to the insides of the envelopes, he wrapped the pieces in tissue paper or coated the insides of the wrappers.

These envelopes were the key for which inventors had been searching. By creating them, Latimer, a self-taught inventor, helped pave the way for every home and business in America and throughout the world to have electric lighting.

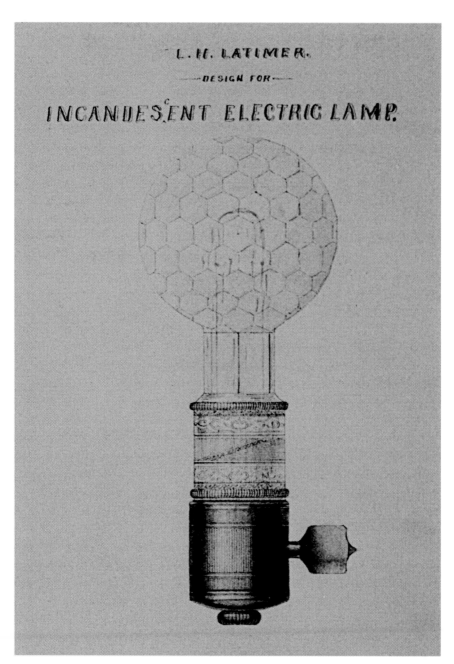

Lewis Latimer's 1880 drawing for an incandescent lamp represents one of the many designs the inventor created.

Lewis Latimer: Born in an Unjust World

This man who made such a contribution to technology was born to parents who had been slaves in the days before the Civil War. Lewis's father, George Latimer, was the son of a white stonemason, Mitchell Latimer, and a black slave, Margaret Olmstead. Mitchell Latimer worked in the Navy Yard at Norfolk, Virginia, and Margaret Olmstead worked as a slave and was owned by Mitchell's brother Edward.

As a child, George lived with his mother at Edward Latimer's home. Apparently Edward died at an early age, and his widow married a man named Edward Mallery.

George later wrote that Mallery treated him well, though the boy worked as a servant. Soon after he turned 16, however, Mallery sent George out to work for a black man named Mich Johnson. George now found that it wasn't only white people who mistreated blacks—Johnson often hit George and gave him only two meals a day.

George worked for Johnson for 14 months. During that time, George was arrested for debts owed by his master, Edward Mallery, and was thrown in jail. At that time, slaves had no rights, and it was not uncommon for them to serve jail time in their masters' place, even though they themselves had not committed any crime. George was released after Mallery paid the charges, but within two weeks he was back in jail, once again for Mallery's debts. This time another man, John Dunson, paid to get George out of jail, perhaps because he wanted George to work for him. From then on, George worked as a slave for a variety of masters, until at last Mallery bought him again. However, once again Mallery sold him, this time to a storekeeper, James B. Gray.

In early 1842, George married Rebecca Smith, who was also a slave. Even though they were married, the newly-weds were not allowed to live together—their owners insisted that they should live where they worked. George and Rebecca were permitted to visit each other only at night after all their chores were done. George had to be back from these visits before sunrise the next morning or he would be beaten severely.

George had often thought of running away, even as a child. He wondered why people were allowed to "own" other people. But whenever he considered leaving, he thought of what would happen if he got caught. Running away from one's owner was very dangerous. Slaves who were caught trying to escape were usually returned to their masters, and were often beaten or treated even more harshly than before their attempted escape. Some runaway slaves were even put to death. Still, freedom from slavery was worth the risk to many, particularly to young men who were strong and daring.

The Latimers Escape North

George Latimer was just such a young man when he and Rebecca decided to try and escape to freedom. There was another reason why they wanted to escape: Rebecca was pregnant, and they were determined that their baby would be born in a northern free state—that is, a state that did not permit slavery. Children born in a slave state—one in which slavery was allowed—could be taken from their parents and sold at auction, like cows or tools. In a free state, it was much more likely that a family could stay together.

George Latimer, pictured here, was the son
of a white stonemason and a black slave.

The Underground Railroad

In the years before the Civil War, abolitionists set up a network to help black slaves escape from the South. This network, called the Underground Railroad, was not an actual train. It was a system of "safe houses" along a route from the southern states to safe places in the North and in Canada. Even though it was not a train, the Underground Railroad used railroad terms. For example, "stations" were safe houses, buildings where fugitive slaves could be kept in secret rooms, attics, or basements. "Conductors" were people who helped guide escaped slaves through the darkness of night along the right routes. And the slaves themselves were known as "freight." It is estimated that more than 50,000 people may have escaped from the South via the Underground Railroad.

During the slavery years, many black slaves managed to escape to the North with the help of the Underground Railroad.

The dividing line between slave states and free states, known as the Mason-Dixon line, ran along the northern borders of Maryland, Virginia, Kentucky, and Arkansas. States to the north of this line were free; those to the south practiced slavery. George and Rebecca hoped to escape from Virginia by boat to Massachusetts, one of the northern free states. Massachusetts was the headquarters of many powerful abolitionists—people who opposed slavery and wanted to see it ended, or abolished. If only he and Rebecca could make it to the city of Boston, George reasoned, they could get help from the abolitionists.

From the minute they stole away from their owners' lands, on October 4, 1842, George and Rebecca Latimer were putting their lives at risk. Traveling at night on deserted roads and hiding at the first sign of civilization, they made their way to the Norfolk seaport, on the Atlantic Ocean. There, they located a northbound ship and sneaked on board.

George and Rebecca headed for the lowest level in the extreme front of the boat. This was where the ship's ballast was kept, the huge pile of rocks and stones used to balance the craft. Here they lingered, trying desperately to stay out of sight. A noise from either one could mean death to them and to their unborn child. So, for all of the nine hours that they lay on the rocks, George and Rebecca had to keep absolutely quiet for fear of being caught.

In Baltimore, Maryland, they left the ship and proceeded by train to New York. Once they were in the North, George and Rebecca were not in as much danger and did not need to hide out as stowaways. George, who had fair skin, pretended to be a wealthy landowner who was traveling with his slave, Rebecca. It took the Latimers four days of traveling like this to reach Massachusetts.

No Guarantee of Freedom

After the difficult trip north from Virginia, Rebecca and George were happy to reach Massachusetts. But, even in that free state, the Latimers were still not truly free. If they were spotted by anyone who recognized them as runaway slaves, they could be returned to their owners in Virginia. Signs like the one below were posted prominently around the city of Boston, warning all African Americans to watch out for slave catchers:

CAUTION!!

COLORED PEOPLE OF BOSTON, one and all, you are hereby respectfully CAUTIONED and advised, to avoid conversing with the Watchmen and Police Officers of Boston…They are empowered to act as KIDNAP-PERS and SLAVE CATCHERS, and they have already been actually employed in Kidnapping, Catching, and Keeping Slaves. Therefore, if you value your Liberty and the Welfare of the Fugitives among you, Shun them in every possible manner, as so many HOUNDS on the track of the most unfortunate of your race.
KEEP A SHARP LOOK OUT FOR KIDNAPPERS,
and have TOP EYE open.

Unknown to George and Rebecca, their owners had placed ads for their capture and return in the Norfolk, Virginia, *Beacon* soon after their escape. The advertisement, which was placed by Mary D. Sayer, Rebecca's owner, offered a $50 reward to the person who returned the runaway slave, and it read as follows:

*RANAWAY from the subscriber last evening, negro woman
REBECCA in the company (as is supposed) with her husband, George Latimer, belonging to Mr. James B. Gray of this
place. She is about 20 years of age, dark mulatto or copper
colored...self-possessed and easy in her manners when
addressed.... All persons are hereby cautioned against har-
boring said slave.*

James Gray placed a similar advertisement in a newspaper calling for the capture and return of "my Negro Man
George, commonly called George Latimer." It described the
runaway man as being five feet three or four inches tall,
about 24 years old, with a "bright yellow" complexion. "He
is of a compact, well made frame, and is rather silent and
slow spoken."

THE JAILING OF GEORGE LATIMER

Unfortunately for George and Rebecca, a man named
William Carpenter was in Boston when they arrived.
Carpenter had once worked for James Gray, and he recog-
nized George the minute that he spotted him on the street.
Wasting no time, he contacted Gray, who arrived on October
18 from Norfolk. Even though he had no proper warrant,
Gray had George Latimer arrested on a false charge of theft
and sent to jail.

Had he been captured in the South, George would have
been turned over to his owner immediately and would likely have suffered a severe beating or other punishment. But
he was more fortunate in Boston. The city was filled with
anti-slavery sympathizers—people who were opposed to

slavery—and word quickly spread of the arrest of George Latimer. Abolitionists were outraged.

Latimer's case was quickly taken on by three prominent Boston lawyers: Charles M. Ellis, Samuel E. Sewall, and Amos B. Merrill. The next day, nearly 300 black supporters—many of whom were former slaves—gathered outside the courthouse in Boston to try and keep James Gray from taking Latimer out of the city. A public meeting was scheduled for October 30 in Boston's famous Faneuil Hall. This historic building had been the scene of many fiery debates leading up to the Revolutionary War and was known as the Cradle of Liberty. Now it would be the scene of an important fight for personal liberty.

Some of the people who showed up for the meeting were supporters of slavery, but many more were abolitionists. Latimer's attorney Samuel Sewall was in charge and opened the meeting with a short speech. There followed a reading of many resolutions—statements of opinion—from those present. One said that "in the person of George Latimer, now confined in Leverett Street jail on the charge of being a slave, are embodied the rights and immunities of all people. . . ." George Latimer's case was to be a test of the rights of all African Americans.

Born
Into
Freedom

The George Latimer case attracted widespread attention. Several protests were planned, and abolitionists stood firmly behind Latimer's cause.

Among them was Frederick Douglass, one of the leaders of the abolitionist movement. Born on a Maryland plantation, Douglass's background was similar to George Latimer's. His father was a white man, his mother a black slave. Douglass, too, had tried to escape from the plantation where he was a slave, but he was captured and thrown in jail. He was then released from jail and sent back to the plantation. As soon as he was able, he escaped to Massachusetts. There, Douglass came in contact with the Massachusetts

Anti-Slavery Society. Through this group, he began making public speeches about slavery and abolition, and he soon became well known. When Douglass heard about George Latimer's plight, it reminded him of his own desperate flight for freedom.

One of America's most famous poets also spoke out in support of Latimer. In 1843, John Greenleaf Whittier wrote a poem that immortalized the Latimers' flight to freedom. In it, he spoke of the masses who gathered in support of Latimer in Boston. The poem, titled "Virginia to Massachusetts," was one of his many anti-slavery poems.

One of the best-known abolitionists was William Lloyd Garrison, a friend of Whittier and the publisher of a Boston newspaper called the *Liberator*. For more than a decade, Garrison had been attacking the practice of slavery in the South. So strongly did Garrison oppose slavery that he encouraged free states to secede, or break away, from the Union—the United States of America.

By now, three more prominent and wealthy men had joined the Latimer cause. William Francis Channing, Frederick Cabot, and Dr. Henry Bowditch started a newspaper called *The Latimer Journal, and North Star*. The first issue was published on November 11, 1842. It sold for one cent per copy. Their goal, said the publishers, was "to meet the urgency of the first enslavement in Boston" as well as to rescue George Latimer from prison. Six issues of the paper were published, and eventually the circulation reached 20,000. It carried the latest news of George Latimer's imprisonment as well as events leading up to the trial and the activities of the abolitionist movement. Although the paper claimed to support no violent measures, even when rescuing slaves, critics claimed that it aroused anger and suspicion.

John Greenleaf Whittier wrote an anti-slavery poem about George and Rebecca Latimer's escape from Virginia to Massachusetts.

During the first week of *The Latimer Journal*'s publication, George Latimer's case was in the forefront of the news in Boston. Abolitionists had started circulating two petitions, asking the sheriff to arrange for Latimer to be discharged from jail. The petitions contained threats against the jail-keeper, Mr. Cooledge, saying that the abolitionists would have him removed from office for abusing his power if Latimer were kept in jail. Upon hearing this, Cooledge, who was working for Gray, Latimer's owner, told Gray that he could no longer be his agent. Samuel Sewall, one of Latimer's lawyers, feared that this might prompt Gray to take Latimer out of jail that very night. Sewall paid a visit to Latimer to warn him what to do if this should happen— "to scream and raise an outcry, and then the negroes would rescue" him. Nearly two dozen black supporters surround-ed the jail that night, but Gray did not arrive.

FREEDOM MUST BE BOUGHT

Unfortunately, the Latimer case did not go as the abolition-ists had hoped. When Justice Lemuel Shaw of the Massachusetts Supreme Court finally handed down his rul-ing in November, it said that George Latimer was still the property of James Gray, who had paid cash for him. Hearing this, Bowditch offered to pay Gray $650, and he accepted. The parties agreed to meet at 7:00 P.M. at the jail to complete the sale. But when the time came and Latimer was released, Bowditch refused to pay the money. He believed that Latimer "would of necessity be rescued [by fellow Negroes, and so] he should not pay anything for him; and thus he backed out of his contract...."

Bowditch's decision to back out of the contract devastated Latimer's backers, for it looked now as if George would be recaptured. Both sides were under a great deal of pressure. At last, in a desperate effort to keep Latimer from being reclaimed by Gray, an African-American minister named Samuel Caldwell made an offer of $400. Gray accepted the offer, and on November 23, 1842, George Latimer became a free man.

That day, *The Latimer Journal, and North Star* proclaimed in its fifth issue, "Latimer is free! What mighty significance is there in these three words! Let them sound from the green hills of Berkshire . . . Let them sound through our whole broad State! Latimer is free!"

Massachusetts: Home of the Free

But the case was not over yet. Citizens who had supported Latimer's cause now took it one step further. Some 65,000 of them signed a petition addressed to the lawmakers of Massachusetts. The petition said they wanted "to free this commonwealth [of Massachusetts] and themselves from all connection with domestic slavery and to secure the citizens of this state from the danger of enslavement..." It asked the lawmakers to do three things:

1. Pass a law prohibiting any officer of the state from holding or arresting any runaway slave;
2. Pass a law making it illegal to hold a runaway slave in a jail or other public property;
3. Suggest changes to the U.S. Constitution that would permanently separate the people of Massachusetts from any connection with slavery.

Slavery in America

Slavery in America was older than the United States itself. The first group of Africans were brought as indentured servants by Dutch traders to the Jamestown Colony in Virginia in 1619, and after that the slave trade grew. In the 1680s, slaves were usually prisoners who had been captured in wars with other African groups and sold to white slave traders or they had been unlucky enough to have been rounded up by slave hunters. Their captors locked them in chains and crammed them into filthy, crowded ships for their trip to the "New World." So bad were the conditions on these ships that many slaves died on the way from lack of food, water, and proper sanitary conditions.

For the first century, the slave trade grew slowly in the American colonies. But as southern plantation owners began growing huge crops of tobacco and cotton, the demand for cheap labor increased. During the eighteenth century, slavery became widespread in the South. George Washington, the first U.S. President, owned slaves. So did Thomas Jefferson, the author of the Declaration of Independence. Slavery became a way of life in the South. Although some slave owners treated their workers with respect, many were cruel and unfair.

In the early 1800s, an anti-slavery movement began in the North, where some states had already voted to abolish slavery. Groups dedicated to freeing slaves and ending slavery in the United States sprang up in northern cities. By 1804, all states to the north of Maryland had agreed to end slavery within their own borders, some

After a time, state lawmakers passed an act supporting the first point. But making changes at the national level was not so easy. Once again, Massachusetts citizens collected signatures on a petition to present to the U.S. Congress. This petition called for "such laws and proposed amendments

immediately, and others in the near future. Just four years later, the United States made importing slaves from other countries illegal. However, the buying and selling of human beings continued within the United States. The American Colonization Society was organized in 1816 to send blacks back to Africa. Although that plan never worked, some free blacks were returned to West Africa, where they founded the country of Liberia—whose name means "free."

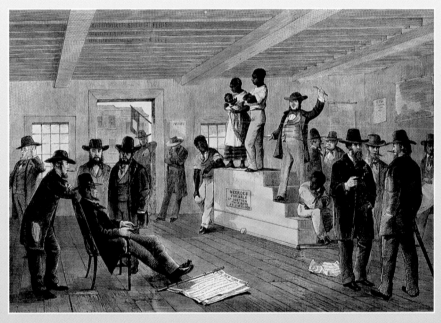

Black families were often split up when their members were sold to different owners at slave auctions.

to the Constitution as should relieve the Commonwealth [of Massachusetts] from all further participation in the crime of oppression." Congress did not approve the idea. But the people had made it clear that they wanted no part of tracking down runaway slaves and returning them to their owners.

The abolitionists had gained a much-needed spokesman back in 1831, when William Lloyd Garrison started his *Liberator* newspaper. The following year, Garrison organized the New England Anti-Slavery Society in Boston and, in 1833, the American Anti-Slavery Society. These groups greatly strengthened the abolitionist cause in the North. Joining Garrison in the movement was the escaped slave Frederick Douglass, who was hired as a speaker by the Massachusetts Anti-Slavery Society. Douglass later took the abolitionist movement to Rochester, New York, where he published *The North Star* newspaper from 1847 to 1860.

Abolitionists were often threatened and in great danger. Elijah Lovejoy, editor of an abolitionist newspaper in Alton, Illinois, was murdered by a group of pro-slavery supporters in 1837. Garrison, too, was dragged through the streets by people who objected to his outspoken stand.

Black workers were the backbone of the economy in the South, and slaveholders were not about to give up their cheap labor without a fight. There were also people in the North who sympathized with the southerners' labor needs and so supported slavery.

FREEDOM . . . AND POVERTY

George and Rebecca Latimer's dream of having their child born into freedom came true soon after they arrived in Massachusetts. George, Jr., was born in 1842, while the issues of his father's trial were still burning. But while the Latimers were delighted by his birth, they worried about how they would support him. Despite George, Sr.'s, extensive experience as a laborer, he had learned that work was very hard to find, particularly for a black man. Feeding the family became even more difficult with the arrival of a second son, William, and a daughter, Margaret, over the next five years.

Lewis, the Latimers' last child, was born on September 4, 1848. It had been six years since George, Sr., had won his freedom, but the family remained desperately poor. Probably no one at the time could have imagined that Lewis, the son of fugitive slaves, born into poverty, would one day become a respected and noted inventor.

Lewis was born in Chelsea, Massachusetts, just outside Boston, where his father operated a barbershop. While he was a baby, the family moved often. They lived in various neighborhoods and eventually moved to Phillips Street, a black neighborhood. Near the Latimers lived the Haydens, whose house was a station on the Underground Railroad. Like George and Rebecca Latimer, the Haydens were escaped slaves. Since their escape, they had devoted their lives to helping other fugitives. Because the Haydens kept close watch for slave catchers or other informers, the Latimers probably felt safe in this neighborhood. For even though George's freedom had been bought, Rebecca was still a fugitive and might be discovered and captured at any time.

George Latimer continued his trade as a barber despite the frequent moves. As soon as he was old enough, Lewis worked in the shop with his dad, sweeping the floors, fetching supplies, and mingling with the customers. When he was not working in the shop, he attended Phillips Grammar School. Lewis was an excellent student, and he showed a particular talent for reading, writing, and drawing. But the family was so poor that he had to work much of the time and could not always attend school.

Freedom Is No Guarantee of Rights

The abolitionist movement grew very strong in the northern United States, thanks to the outspokenness of people like Frederick Douglass and William Lloyd Garrison. Yet the country as a whole remained stubbornly supportive of slavery. Abolitionists had hoped that the support shown for George Latimer during his imprisonment would greatly strengthen their position. But many setbacks to a slave-free society still lay ahead. For one thing, freed slaves like Latimer and Douglass were discovering that, for a black person in America, legal freedom did not guarantee that he or she would be treated fairly. Freedom did not mean equality.

In 1850, Congress passed the Fugitive Slave Act. This law allowed federal government agents to capture runaway slaves anywhere in the United States and return them to their owners. The first such laws had been passed in 1793, but the Fugitive Slave Act was even more strict than the earlier ones.

A further move to deny blacks their rights involved the Supreme Court case of the slave Dred Scott. Scott's owner had moved him from the slave state (where slavery was legal) of Missouri into the free states (where slavery was against the law) of Illinois and Wisconsin before moving back to Missouri. In his case, Scott claimed that his time on free soil made him a free man. Abolitionists rallied behind him, hoping that his case would pave the way for an end to slavery. But the Supreme Court's 1857 decision went against them. In it, the justices tried to interpret the feelings of America's founding fathers. They decided:

- that black men and women had no rights that whites were bound to respect,
- that [blacks] could not become citizens of the United States, and
- that Congress had no power to exclude slavery from any part of U.S. territory....

As unfair as these rulings seem today, they did serve one good purpose: Abolitionists were now so outraged that they became more determined than ever to fight for an end to slavery.

Dred Scott, a slave, said he deserved freedom because
he had been taken by his master into a free state.

At night, Lewis also helped his father in his paperhanging business, one of the many trades that George Latimer pursued. Long hours of working together gave father and son a good chance to know each other, and also helped Lewis to become quite expert as a paper hanger. In addition to his other jobs, Lewis also sold copies of the *Liberator* newspaper. Not only did the youngster earn money by selling the newspaper, he also learned a great deal about the abolitionist movement.

A Family Divided

Looking back on his life many years later, Lewis Latimer greatly valued the time that he had spent working with his father. Those years would be his only memory of George Sr. When Lewis was ten years old, his father left his wife and children. No one knows why he left. He may have been depressed by his inability to support his family. Perhaps George Latimer thought that his life as an outspoken abolitionist was endangering Rebecca and their children. The Fugitive Slave Act of 1850 was a peril to Rebecca. Since no one had paid for her freedom, she was still a fugitive slave. George may have worried that because of him, Rebecca would be caught and returned to Virginia. Or he may have been nervous about his own status—even though his supporters had paid for his freedom, George had no legal papers to prove that he was free. If he were caught without such papers, he could be returned to slavery at once.

Whatever the reason for her husband's leaving, Rebecca could not support her family alone. The two older sons were sent to the Farm School in western Massachusetts, more than 80 miles from Boston. This was a state-run school where students could learn a skill or trade by working with an experienced person—a sort of apprentice program. The school provided room and board and some payment for the students' services. The Latimers' daughter, Margaret, went to live with a friend. But for the time being, young Lewis stayed at home with his mother.

Rebecca Latimer was offered a job as a stewardess on a ship in about 1858, however, so Lewis was sent to the Farm School to join his brothers. Both of the older boys hated the school, and it was not very long before Lewis shared their feelings. Upon his arrival, he found out that George, Jr., had been sent to work for a farmer and that William was apprenticed to a hotel keeper in Springfield, Massachusetts. With both brothers away, Lewis stayed at the school alone for more than two years. At last, William returned from living in Springfield, and he was delighted to find that Lewis was still there.

The boys immediately began plotting their escape from the school. Their plan involved jumping onto a train and hiding in the railroad cars until they reached Boston. Begging for food along the way, they ran, walked, and sneaked onto trains.

When they finally reached Boston in 1860, it only took a few days for them to discover that their mother had returned from her job at sea. A happy reunion followed, which included a great deal of catching up on one another's lives after having been separated for nearly three years. Despite the fact that Rebecca had little money and was still living in fear of being caught and returned to slavery, she promised her sons that she would provide a home for them until they could find work.

CHAPTER THREE

NEEDED: AN OFFICE BOY WITH "A TASTE FOR DRAWING"

Work for young men that paid a decent wage was not easy to find in mid-nineteenth-century Boston. For a time after his escape from the Farm School, Lewis Latimer waited tables in Boston. Next, he took a job with a family in Roxbury, a suburb of Boston, doing odd jobs. But this restless 13-year-old with an active mind was not content to do manual work. His formal schooling had ended at age ten, but Lewis continued to educate himself. Longing for a job that posed some mental challenge, he applied at the office of Isaac Wright, a well-known Boston lawyer. Wright hired him, and Lewis worked in his office for more than two years, building a fine reputation for himself.

War Clouds Form over the Union

Soon after Lewis started to work at the law office, clouds of war began to gather over the United States. The conflict between southern slaveholders and northern abolitionists had been growing more tense every year.

In 1860, Abraham Lincoln, who opposed slavery, was elected President of the United States. Upset that a man who was not supportive of slavery now held the nation's highest office, South Carolina decided to secede from the Union. Florida, Georgia, Alabama, Mississippi, Louisiana, and Texas soon followed. Together, they formed the Confederate States of America.

War Between the States

The Civil War—the bloodiest war ever fought on American soil—erupted on April 12, 1861, when Confederate troops fired the first shots at Fort Sumter, South Carolina. The issue of slavery, which had so long divided the country, was now coming to a climax.

The South, made up of states that were in favor of slavery, did not want Abraham Lincoln to be President. Lincoln disliked slavery. Although he was not exactly an abolitionist, he was against extending slavery into new states entering the Union. But slavery was not the only reason that the war began. Lincoln was absolutely determined to keep the nation whole. So when southern states seceded and their troops fired on Fort Sumter, a Union fort in Confederate territory, Lincoln called out the militia. The Civil War had begun.

Needed: An Office Boy with "a Taste for Drawing"

The Emancipation Proclamation

In August 1862, Lincoln wrote to *The New York Tribune*, saying: "My paramount object in this struggle is to save the Union, and is not either to save or to destroy slavery. If I could save the Union without freeing any slave I would do it; and if I could save it by freeing all the slaves I would do it; and if I could save it by freeing some and leaving others alone, I would also do that."

Later that year, Lincoln chose the third option when he wrote one of the most famous documents of his career. The Emancipation Proclamation was a cornerstone of freedom for African Americans. This order, which went into effect on January 1, 1863, freed all slaves then living in the Confederate states. It did not free slaves living in the border states of Missouri, Kentucky, and Maryland—slave states that had remained loyal to the Union. Nor did it free slaves living in certain sections or counties of the South that were still under the control of the Union. The Proclamation also allowed African Americans to join the Union Army, something that had previously been prohibited. By this point in the war, however, the Union badly needed soldiers.

Abraham Lincoln wrote in the Proclamation: " . . . I do order and declare that all persons held as slaves within said designated States and parts of States are, and henceforward shall be, free; and that the [U.S. government] . . . will recognize and maintain the freedom of said persons." The Emancipation Proclamation freed only about 200,000 slaves during the war, but it was a tremendous step forward in the fight for black rights.

Shortly after Abraham Lincoln signed the Emancipation Proclamation, the Latimer brothers went to war on the side of the Union. William entered the navy, and George, Jr., joined the 29th Connecticut Army Regiment. At age 16,

Lewis was too young to enlist legally, but he didn't let his age stop him. No one challenged him when he lied about his birth date, and on September 16, 1864, he became a cabin boy aboard the U.S.S. *Massasoit*. This vessel was a sidewheel gunboat, part of a fleet whose job was to protect Union ships sailing between New York and Virginia. Another part of the *Massasoit*'s duty was to keep Confederate boats from reaching the coasts of northern states. During Lewis's time aboard, the ship was involved in fighting on the James River in Virginia and at a place called Howellett's House.

Just three days before Confederate leader Robert E. Lee surrendered at Appomattox Court House on April 9, 1865, the *Massasoit* received orders to carry a series of top-secret

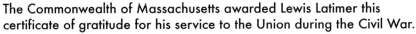

The Commonwealth of Massachusetts awarded Lewis Latimer this certificate of gratitude for his service to the Union during the Civil War.

Needed: An Office Boy with "a Taste for Drawing"

messages to William Tecumseh Sherman. Sherman was the Union general who had captured the city of Atlanta, Georgia, and many other key spots in the South. By now, Sherman was fighting in North Carolina, and here the *Massasoit* stayed until the end of the war.

On July 3, 1865, Lewis Latimer was honorably discharged from the service and went home to Boston. Later, he received a certificate from the Commonwealth of Massachusetts that expressed "the people's gratitude for your patriotism."

TESTING THE PROMISE OF FREEDOM

Although he was not yet legally an adult when the war ended, Latimer had carried the weight and responsibilities of a man for some time. Back in Boston, he and his mother found a new place to live on Phillips Street. Records show that Lewis's father was in town during the war years, but the family never saw him. Some historians believe that although George, Sr., never made contact with them, he was nevertheless keeping an eye on his wife and children.

If George Latimer's reason for avoiding his family was because he feared being taken back into slavery or endangering his wife in that way, those fears should have ended with the passage of the Thirteenth Amendment to the U.S. Constitution. On December 18, 1865, the amendment became effective across the United States. "Neither slavery nor involuntary servitude, shall exist within the United States, or any place subject to their jurisdiction," it read. Slavery had ended, at last. Yet even after the passage of the Thirteenth Amendment, for some unknown reason George, Sr., chose not to make contact with his family.

After the Civil War, certain southern states passed Black Codes, which supposedly protected the rights of African Americans to "marry, own property, travel, work for pay, and sue in court." But in actuality, the codes, or laws, severely limited black rights. For instance, the codes said that black people could marry—but they could marry only other blacks. They were also not paid fair wages, were not treated equally in the justice system, and could buy property only on the rare occasions that white people would sell to them.

In the North, factory owners saw former slaves as a source of cheap labor. They took advantage of them. In turn, white workers then resented blacks because they saw them as competition for their own jobs. Thus, on paper, black rights had been assured. But in reality, America was a long way from justice.

"A Taste for Drawing"

Like his father, Lewis Latimer, now 17 years old, soon found that it was not easy for a black man to get respectable work that paid well. Nevertheless, he vowed that he would find an interesting job. He wanted work that promised him a chance to advance as he gained experience. After much frustration, he found it: a job advertised for an office boy who had "a taste for drawing." It was a job that was just right for Lewis, who had an intense interest in and talent for drawing. He applied and was given the job. It paid $3.00 per week, which was less than a white man would have earned but was considered a good wage for a young black worker.

Crosby and Gould was a company of patent lawyers. These were attorneys who helped inventors prepare and

Needed: An Office Boy with "a Taste for Drawing"

Latimer's sketch of his bedroom in 1872 was evidence of his drawing skills.

file the complicated legal forms that were necessary for patent protection so that no one could copy or steal their ideas. When the forms were sent to the U.S. Patent Office, in Washington, D.C., a technical drawing of the object or invention—and often a working model of it—accompanied the patent applications. It was a patent attorney's job to help inventors progress through each stage of the complicated patent application process.

The Reality of Injustice

On July 28, 1868, what should have been another landmark in African-American history took place. That was the passage of the Fourteenth Amendment to the U.S. Constitution. This amendment, or formal change to the Constitution, contains several sections. The first one had to do with the rights of U.S. citizens. It was now illegal for any state to "make or enforce any law which will abridge [limit] the privileges or immunities of citizens of the United States." It also prohibited states from depriving " . . . any person of life, liberty or property, without due process of law. . . . " Finally, it said that all citizens were to have "equal protection of the laws." The Fourteenth Amendment was supposed to guarantee that African Americans had the same rights and protections as other citizens. But in everyday life, blacks continued to be treated differently from other citizens.

Many historians felt that the failure of the Fourteenth Amendment to protect the rights of African Americans led to the adoption of the Fifteenth Amendment, in 1870. This amendment guaranteed that a person's right to vote would not be endangered because of "race, color, or previous condition of servitude." On paper, the Fifteenth Amendment seemed to be a step forward for black rights. Yet, like the Black Codes, there were so many problems and restrictions attached to the new freedom that few black men actually took advantage of their new right to vote (women did not yet have the right). It was still far from a just world for African Americans.

In the days before and during the Civil War, the number of patent applications that were approved by the U.S. Patent Office was small. In the 1860s, only about 8,000 patents were issued each year. But in the next decade, more than 12,000 patents per year were granted. In order to keep up with the increased amount of work, Crosby and Gould needed more

Needed: An Office Boy with "a Taste for Drawing"

drafters. These were the people who made the technical drawings that were submitted with the applications to the Patent Office in Washington, D.C.

Lewis Latimer was an office boy, not a drafter, but he was very anxious to learn the trade. For weeks, he carefully watched the drafters as they worked, and he noted the kinds of tools that they used. Their drawings fascinated the young man, and he was determined to teach himself these skills. So he purchased some used books on drafting, and he bought a used set of drafting tools. Thus armed, he began the challenging process of educating himself. Every day after work, Latimer would practice with his tools and read his collection of books. After several weeks of study, he felt certain enough of his skills to approach one of the drafters at Crosby and Gould. He asked if he could do some drawings for him.

At first, the drafter laughed, but he finally agreed to let Latimer give it a try. The drafter was astounded to see that a young office boy with little schooling or training could create drawings of such high quality. Occasionally, he began to let Latimer help him with his work.

Eventually, the boss saw Latimer's work; he was so impressed that he let Latimer do drafting every day. The boss then offered him a position as drafter and raised his pay. Lewis Latimer's hard work and many hours of study had paid off.

GETTING AHEAD IN AN UNFAIR WORLD

As Latimer's drafting skills improved, he rose in the ranks at Crosby and Gould. After many years, he became head drafter. In that position, he earned $20.00 per week. This

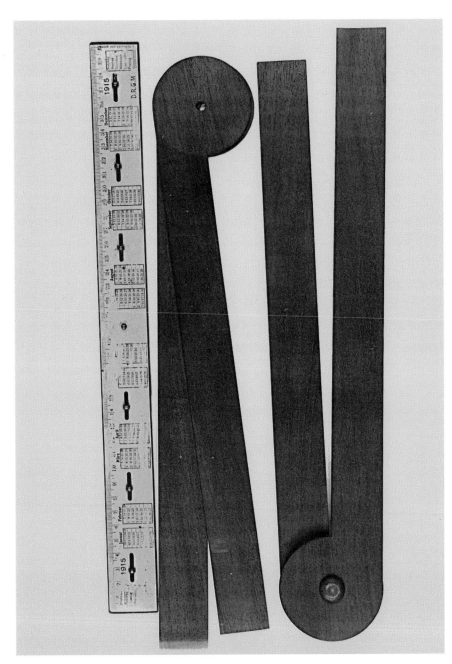

While working at Crosby and Gould, Latimer bought a set
of used drafting tools and taught himself how to use them.

was not a bad wage, but it was $5.00 less per week than a white person in the same position would make. Latimer, like many black workers of his day, thus found himself the victim of wage discrimination. Although he was respected by his fellow workers throughout his career, Latimer's salary was almost always less than that of whites who performed the same duties.

As head drafter, Latimer supervised the building of working models of inventions. Inventors submitted these models with their applications to the U.S. Patent Office. In addition to being chief drafter, the partners of the firm trusted Latimer so much that when they needed to be out of town, they left the office in his charge. For more than 11 years, Latimer maintained a fine relationship with the firm of Crosby and Gould, laying the foundation for the inventor that he himself would one day become.

"Ebon Venus"

Let others boast of maidens fair,
Of eyes blue and golden hair,
My heart, like needle ever true,
Turns to the maid of ebon hue.
I love her form of matchless grace,
The dark brown beauty of her face,
Her lips that speak of love's delight,
Her eyes that gleam as stars at night.
O'er marble Venus let them rage,
Who set the fashions of the age;
Each to his taste, but as for me,
My Venus shall be ebony.

This tender tribute, entitled "Ebon Venus," was written by Lewis Latimer for a young woman who had become very important in his life. Mary Wilson was from Fall River, a city about 50 miles from Boston. Mary seems to have been well

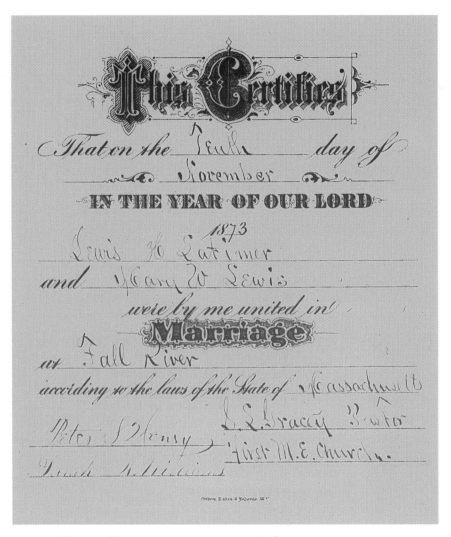

Mary Wilson and Lewis Latimer were married in late 1873, as this marriage certificate shows.

educated, although little is known about her and her family. What *is* known, however, is that Latimer was very much in love with her. He found an outlet for his love in poetry.

On November 10, 1873, Mary and Lewis were married. The two had much in common and would enjoy a long and very loving marriage. Mary Latimer always took a keen interest in her husband's career and encouraged him to study and better himself throughout his life.

In truth, Latimer did not need much encouragement. He was very highly motivated and loved to learn. He put his talents to work not only as a poet but as an artist. In his spare time, he liked to draw and paint. The skills that he developed through his art projects also helped him to become a better drafter.

Mary Wilson Latimer

WORKING NEAR THE GREATS

By the time he was 27, Latimer had an excellent reputation with Crosby and Gould. Just one block from the office on School Street in Boston was the laboratory of Alexander Graham Bell, a Scottish-born inventor who would soon make history himself. For many years, Bell had worked with hearing-impaired people, helping them to learn different ways of communicating. It was natural that Bell would work with the hearing-impaired—his own mother was nearly deaf, and his father was a speech teacher who had created a visual system of communication for the deaf.

When he was not busy teaching, Bell was working on his inventions. By 1874, he was developing a device to change people's voices into electrical impulses and transmit them over a wire. He was aided in his experiments by a 20-year-old electronics expert, Thomas Watson. On June 2, 1875, Bell was successful. The sound that he transmitted was even better than he had hoped. Instead of being just an electrical impulse, its tone varied like a human voice. Bell realized then that it would be only a short time until he figured out how to transmit human voices correctly.

Even though he was impatient to continue his experiments, Bell knew that he must patent this unique device at once in order to keep his idea protected from imitation or theft. But, like many other inventors, he found that filing a patent application was a terribly time-consuming and tedious process. To get some help on making the drawings necessary for the application, he went down the street to Crosby and Gould. There he met the company's chief drafter, Lewis Latimer.

Latimer was assigned to prepare the drawings and help write the descriptions that would accompany the patent application. Just which application (or applications) Latimer worked on for Bell is unclear—Bell was granted several patents from 1875 to 1880, many of which had something or other to do with the telephone.

Getting the applications submitted on time was critical. Many inventors were working on telephone-related devices. If any one of them filed an application earlier, Bell would not get credit for his ideas. In 1874, inventor Elisha Gray had patented a device much like Bell's, in England. Now Gray was applying for a U.S. patent. Fortunately for Bell, Latimer worked quickly and efficiently. The patent application, with its finely drawn illustrations and descriptive text, was filed just before Gray submitted his. A series of lawsuits followed in which Gray tried to show that his patent should be the one granted. But in the end, the U.S. Supreme Court awarded the patent for the electromagnetic transmitter and receiver to Alexander Graham Bell.

On March 7, 1876, Bell was issued his patent. Thanks to Latimer's dedication and talent, the complicated paperwork had been completed on time. If it had not, the name Bell might not be associated with telephones today. Many years after his death, the Alliance of Black Telecommunication Employees of AT&T (American Telephone and Telegraph Company) honored Latimer as the man who did some of the original drawings of Bell's most famous invention.

Igniting the Creative Spark

Working on so many patent applications for other inventors ignited a spark in Latimer's soul. He enjoyed drafting as well as preparing patent applications. He was inspired by the great minds of the people with whom he worked, and he found their inventions exciting. Exposure to the inventors gave Latimer some ideas of his own.

Two years before working with Bell, Latimer had received a patent on a project titled "Improvement of Water Closets." (A water closet is another term for a toilet.) With a partner, C. W. Brown, Latimer had made changes to the toilets on trains. It was not unusual that the two would be working on an improvement of an existing device. Most patent applications then filed were not for new inventions. Instead, they were variations or refinements of things already invented.

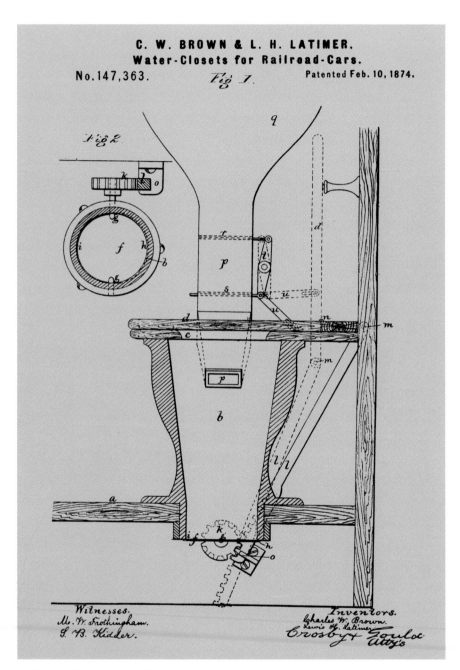

Latimer's first patent—for an improved train
toilet—was registered on February 10, 1874.

The old-style toilets, as Latimer and Brown noted in their application, were in need of improvement.

Instead of the old-style train toilets, which were open directly through to the outdoors, Latimer and Brown developed a pivoted bottom. When the lid of the toilet was raised for use, the pivoted bottom closed automatically, shutting out wind and debris from the outdoors. When a person closed the lid after using the device, the pivoted area opened to allow the unit to flush. This design was used on train-car toilets well into the twentieth century. It was registered as patent number 147,363 by Latimer and Brown on February 10, 1874. This patent marked the first of many useful devices that Lewis Latimer would refine or invent.

Tireless Energy and Determination

Latimer's life thus far had been filled not only with success but also with obstacles. Since childhood, he had had to work extremely hard for any advancement. Nothing in his life had been easy or assured. In learning how to overcome obstacles, however, Latimer developed a strong sense of persistence and determination. It seemed that nothing could keep him from following a path that he wanted to take or from developing what he thought was a good idea. In addition to his own strong character, he also had the support and encouragement of his wife.

His restless energy, coupled with a constant desire to broaden his mind, may have been part of the reason why Latimer decided, after 11 years, to end his employment with Crosby and Gould. A more practical reason for leaving may have been changes within the company. By 1879, Crosby had retired and Gould had died. A new partner, George W. Gregory, joined the firm, but he and Latimer did not get along very well.

There was also an economic recession going on in Boston at that time. Many companies found themselves with less work than in previous years. This made it difficult for workers to find or hold jobs. For a time, Lewis worked with another patent lawyer, Joseph Adams, whose office was just down the street from Crosby and Gould. But their work was scarce, and soon Latimer was forced to take a job at the Esterbrook Iron Foundry, in south Boston. This company made patterns or molds into which iron could be poured to make manhole covers, grates, and similar items. This job did not last long either, and within a few months, Latimer was out of work.

Not one to be defeated or discouraged, Latimer decided to follow his sister Margaret's advice and move to Bridgeport, Connecticut, where she was living with her husband, Augustus Hawley. Bridgeport was not in an economic recession, as Latimer would soon discover. Instead, it was a prosperous, bustling industrial city, located on the shore of Long Island Sound.

Mary and Lewis moved to Bridgeport in 1879, shortly after Lewis turned 31 years old. In an interview with the local newspaper, he discussed his pleasure with his new home and his surprise that such a vibrant urban center could exist so close to New York City.

Bridgeport had many factories, which produced everything from ladies' corsets to sewing machines. And there was no shortage of inventors living here, a fact that naturally excited Latimer. Still, when he began the search for a job, he was very disappointed. At the time, it seemed that no one in Bridgeport needed someone with either drafting or patent application skills. But the Latimers needed an income on which to live, and so Lewis turned to the trade that his father had taught him so many years earlier—wallpaper hanging.

An Introduction to Electric Lighting

With his usual determination, Latimer still continued his search for a job in his chosen field. Soon he was successful, taking a position as a technical drafter at the Follandsbee Machine Shop.

While working at Follandsbee, Latimer's life took a turn that would lead him into the field of electricity. Not long after he started in his new position, a man came into the shop who already had a reputation as an able inventor. His name was Hiram Maxim. Among Maxim's most notable accomplishments in his lifetime was creating the first fully automatic machine gun, an innovation that proved very successful in warfare. Maxim was a talented inventor of many interests. He was even experimenting with an airplane at the same time as the Wright brothers were. His model used a steam-powered engine, however, which was too heavy to allow the aircraft to lift off the ground.

Wandering into Follandsbee's, Maxim approached the table where Lewis Latimer was working on a drawing. Maxim watched him for some time. Finally, he said that he had never seen an African-American drafter. Maxim asked Latimer how he had learned the craft. Latimer explained in his modest way that he was self-taught, that he had studied and practiced on his own while working as an office boy

Edison's Rival, Hiram Maxim

In the late 1870s, Hiram Maxim was Thomas Alva Edison's most serious rival in the field of electric lighting. Maxim, like Edison and a number of other inventors, was busy experimenting with many different types of filaments, hoping eventually to find an inexpensive and long-lasting one.

Maxim had a great deal of experience with arc lighting, and he had applied for two patents in that field. By late 1880, his two-year-old United States Electric Light Company, which specialized in arc lighting, employed 20 workers.

To broaden his knowledge, Maxim had gone to Menlo Park, New Jersey, to talk with Edison about the making of filaments and lamps. He was impressed by the inventor's successes, but Edison had paid little attention to Maxim's work. Edison did not have a good understanding of human nature, and it was difficult for him to work closely with other people.

Maxim went about inventing with a flair that attracted more attention than that given to his famous rival. Once, at a demonstration in New York City, where hundreds of people could see his work, Maxim set up a display of his lamps. One of them burned brightly for 24 hours without showing signs of failure, a very impressive achievement at that time.

Edison didn't comment. The inventor had a reputation for being conceited about his accomplishments and slow to share credit. He even claimed to be suspicious of any procedure or product designed by another person. Comparing the two inventors, *Illustrated Science News* wrote, "In connection with electric illumination, [Hiram Maxim's] name will be remembered long after that of his boastful rival [Thomas Edison] is forgotten." However, history did not allow that to happen.

Right: Hiram Maxim, head of United States Electric Lighting Company, hoped to find a filament that would provide long-lasting lamp light.

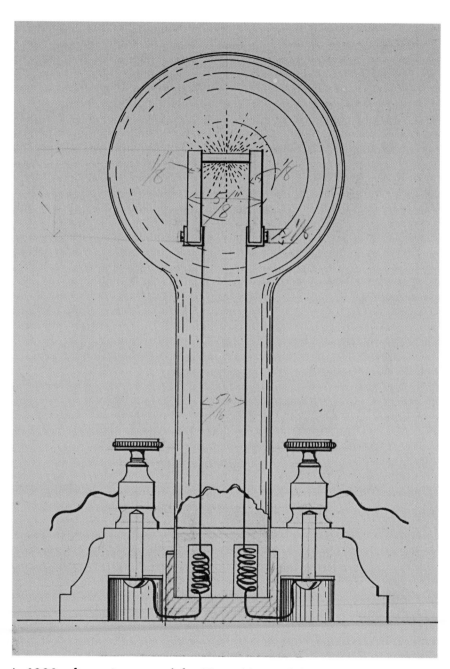

In 1880, after going to work for Hiram Maxim, Latimer developed this design for an electric lightbulb.

Lewis Latimer

at Crosby and Gould in Boston. In an amazing coincidence, it turned out that Maxim had worked there once himself. He was both surprised and impressed to hear that Latimer had held the position of chief drafter.

Hiram Maxim was quick to recognize talent, and he saw in Lewis Latimer a great asset to Maxim's young firm— United States (or U.S.) Electric Lighting Company. Maxim was the company's chief engineer. Within a week, Latimer was working for Maxim as a drafter and as Maxim's private secretary. He began the work of familiarizing himself with electric incandescent light construction and operation. Over the years, Hiram Maxim's United States Electric Lighting Company made major contributions to the new field of electricity. And many of those contributions were thanks to the new, young, and eager drafter whom Maxim had hired in 1880.

LIGHTING
UP THE
WORLD

The decade of the 1880s was truly an exciting time to be involved in electricity. Newspapers and journals across the country carried stories of the latest developments by the many inventors working on bulbs, filaments, and lamps.

Lewis Latimer was thrilled to be a part of the excitement. True to his nature, immediately after being hired by Maxim, Latimer set out to teach himself all he could about this new field. A quick student, he was determined to make a place for himself.

As an African American and a self-educated son of slaves, Latimer faced special challenges, but he was not discouraged from pursuing his dreams. Never once did he think of himself as a second-class citizen. He was determined to learn and to accomplish his goals.

Making His Way

Latimer's hard work was rewarded when, soon after he went to work for Hiram Maxim's company, he was chosen as a member of Bridgeport's Scientific Society. This was a group of leading scientists and inventors to which Maxim himself belonged.

In 1880, the same year that Latimer was hired, the United States Electric Lighting Company moved its headquarters to Brooklyn, New York. Anxious to take the lead in this highly competitive field, the company's managers urged their employees to experiment with their own ideas and test inventions on which they might be working. Maxim himself, however, did not support this idea. (Latimer believed that Maxim was jealous of his workers' inventive talents.)

Maxim's attitude, however, did not stop Latimer or other employees from experimenting. Latimer was working on several different ideas. He was experimenting with designs for equipment used in the manufacture of lightbulbs. One of these was an oven in which to bake filaments. Another involved a chemical that was used to create the vacuum inside the bulb and thus lengthen the life of the filament. He even developed a plan for building glassblowing equipment that could be used in making lightbulbs. Among Latimer's more interesting inventions that were not patented were a new switch for turning lights on and off and a more efficient light socket.

Latimer, however, patented three ideas while working for the United States Electric Lighting Company. One was a wooden base for arc lamps, which he developed with a partner, John Tregoning. A few of these wooden bases can still be

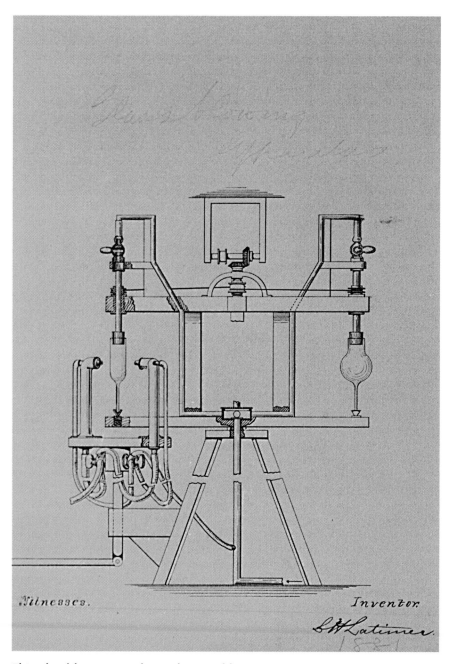

This glassblowing machine, designed by Latimer,
simplified the production of lightbulbs.

seen today in the William T. Hammer Collection of antique electrical devices. They have been displayed at the Smithsonian Institution and other important museums across the United States. As was often the case in those days, Latimer and Tregoning were never credited for their ideas because they had developed them while at work. It was expected that their employers would get the credit—and the profits, if any were to be made.

The Race for a Better Filament

The United States Electric Lighting Company was one of the main competitors in the great race to develop a better filament for the incandescent lightbulb. And it was Latimer's ideas that helped put the company at the forefront of that race. One of those ideas was a new plan for attaching the carbonized filament to the wires that carried electricity from the base of the lamp to the bulb. The other was a new method of building filaments. Latimer would later patent each of these methods.

Until now, the big problem with filaments had been that the carbon pieces broke easily or became twisted during use. Latimer solved this problem by putting the "blanks"—shapes from which the carbon filaments were made—inside tiny cardboard envelopes. The blanks were wrapped in tissue paper to prevent them from sticking to the envelopes. The envelopes did not trap the paper or wood, which would have caused the carbonized material to break. Instead, they expanded or contracted along with the filament material.

The "Process of Manufacturing Carbons" was how Latimer's newest patent application was headed, and it

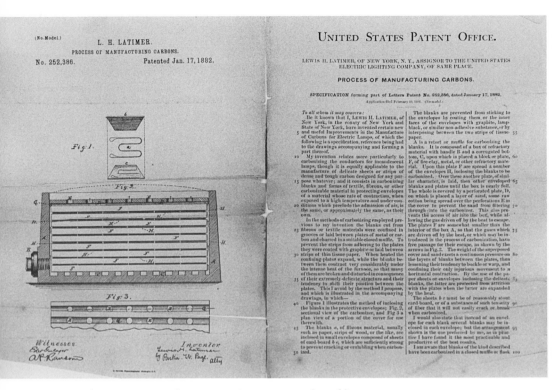

Patent documentation for Latimer's unique carbon-filament manufacturing process included detailed drawings by the inventor.

was filed on February 19, 1881. It was this invention that paved the way for the development of the long-lasting, inexpensive lightbulb.

As occurred with his other inventions, however, Latimer did not receive the credit—and the profits—directly. Inventors were expected to assign their patents to the company, which Latimer did as soon as it was granted, on January 17, 1882. As a result of this practice, we may never know just how many of Lewis Latimer's inventions were used by the United States Electric Lighting Company.

One of Latimer's inventions that *is* known to have been adopted by the United States Electric Lighting Company, however, was the lamp that he developed in partnership with Joseph V. Nichols. It was patented in February 1881. This new device, which used an improved method for connecting the filament to the lead wires, was quickly named the Maxim electric lamp, after the owner of the company. There is no record that Latimer objected to his invention being claimed by his employer. In fact, he even worked hard to promote the new lamp.

This is how Lewis Latimer's device became the Maxim lamp, and why the new filament was used in the project. Curiously, however, it was formed into an M-shaped design!

Because Hiram Maxim owned the company for which Latimer worked, Latimer's lightbulb was named the Maxim lamp.

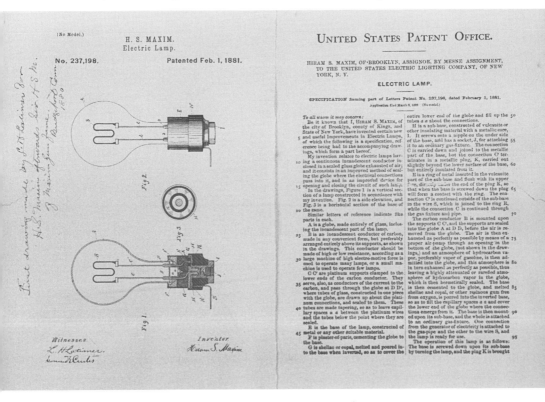

Bringing Electricity to the People

At the United States Electric Lighting Company, Lewis Latimer was given the job of helping city governments set up electric light plants and install wiring in public buildings and along streets. Experiments had proven that it was better to wire streetlights in parallel circuits, rather than in series. When one bulb wired in a series burned out, the whole string went dark, and it took much trial and error to find the bad bulb. But when streetlights were wired in parallel circuits, if one bulb failed, the others continued to burn.

Latimer's first such project was to supervise the installation of lighting in many large buildings in New York City. Among them were the Equitable Insurance Company, the Union Club, and the Fisk and Hatch building. After successfully completing these projects, he was sent to Philadelphia, Pennsylvania, where he helped wire the offices of the newspaper *The Ledger.*

Latimer's greatest challenge was working in the Canadian city of Montreal, in the province of Quebec. When Latimer arrived, he found that most of the people who were to help him on the project spoke only French. How was he to communicate with them well enough to accomplish the job? Hundreds of technical details must be made absolutely clear to them, or the project would end in failure.

As usual, Latimer rose to the challenge: He taught himself French. Each night, he prepared detailed lists of instructions and directions for the workers to follow the next day. After writing the instructions in English, he would work with one of the clerks to do a careful translation into French. In this way, he could communicate with his workers in French about the specifics of the jobs they were to do. The Canadians were very impressed by Latimer's efforts to work with them in their own language.

Off to London

Latimer learned quickly. As his knowledge of electricity reached new heights, he was named chief electrical engineer for the United States Electric Lighting Company. He was one of the few people in the company who knew all phases of lamp manufacturing. So, when advice was needed on setting up a lamp factory in London, England, the company sent Latimer to do the job.

The factory was to be a part of the British Maxim-Weston Electric Light Company. By now, Hiram Maxim was no longer actively working with the United States Electric Lighting Company. Instead, he was spending most of his time working on refining the machine gun that he had developed. But his partner Edward Weston—another successful electrical inventor who later founded the Weston Electrical Instrument Company in New Jersey—became quite active in the London company.

Mary Latimer accompanied Lewis on the London trip. They sailed on the ship *Ancoria* in late 1881, arriving in London on New Year's Day 1882.

Mary spent her days in London writing letters, crocheting, going for walks and shopping, and studying German. Lewis's time was not entirely taken up with work. Mary wrote in her journal about the two of them and an associate going to the Crystal Palace to see an electrical exhibition. The work of many inventors was displayed there, including that of Thomas Alva Edison. But there was much about England, such as the gloomy weather, that she did not like.

Latimer, too, was not entirely happy in England working with the British. His job was to teach the workers how to make carbon filaments and lightbulbs, using his own process. He was an excellent teacher, but he felt that the British resented his presence. They made it clear to him that they did not want to take orders from an American—and particularly not from a black American.

It was obvious, though, that Latimer understood his business, for the job was completed in just nine months—three months ahead of schedule. The factory was a success, but Lewis did not view the experience with fondness. "In London," he wrote in his journal, "I was in hot water from the day I came until I returned."

This feeling was part of the reason why the Latimers planned to leave England as soon as his work was done. Another factor was Mary's discontent. Even though she had her dear "Lew," as she called him, Mary was homesick. Trying to hide this fact from her husband was impossible. Although he tried to make her visit as pleasant as possible—he even took her across the English Channel to visit Paris—they were both ready to return to the United States.

During their time in London, Latimer worked on the drawings for another invention. Mary referred to it in her journal as "some improvement in elevators." What Latimer had improved was the suspension system by which the elevator hung from its cable. Mary took a strong interest in the project and hoped for its success.

Unfortunately, Mary Latimer did not get her wish. Lewis made many changes and improvements on his design over the next several years. He continued working on it even after

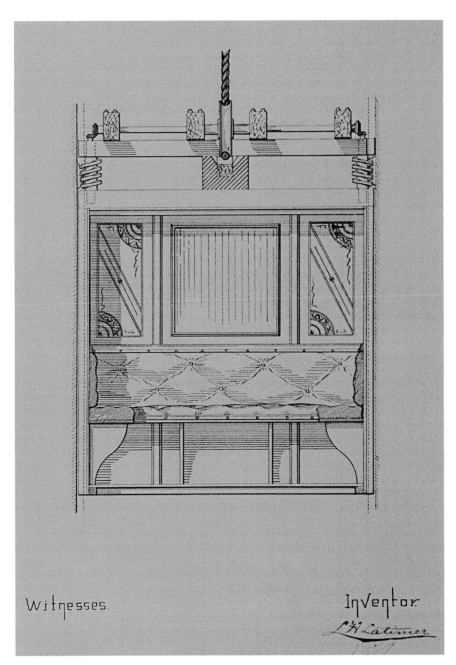

Witnesses.

Inventor

L.H. Latimer

Latimer was not able to convince companies to adapt
his improvements to the suspension system for elevators.

they returned to the United States. He visited with Otis, Westinghouse, and General Electric—all companies that designed and built elevators—but they had little interest in his invention.

A Time of Change

Back home, Latimer found disappointment of another kind. Maxim had stayed in England to continue working on his gun, and he had no plans to return to the United States. Without his leadership, the United States Electric Lighting Company had changed considerably. It had changed so much, in fact, that Latimer found himself unemployed after returning to New York late in 1882. His future looked grim.

Such a talented man as Latimer was not to be out of a job for long, however. He soon found work in Brooklyn as a drafter with the Olmstead Lighting Company. After a short time, he was put in charge of the division that manufactured lamps. Unfortunately, that company went out of business soon after Latimer joined the firm, so he was forced to look for work again. He found it at the Acme Electric Company in New York City.

It was while he was employed at Acme that Lewis began work on the Latimer lamp. At that time, many inventors were working on various types of lamps. (During the 1880s, several thousand lamp patents may have been issued to different inventors.) Latimer himself developed several different types of lamps. One was an arc lamp; another was a multiple-carbon incandescent lamp. Broken carbon filaments were a big problem in early lamps, but this one used several carbons and offered an easy way to replace them when they broke. Latimer is probably best known for the incandescent electric lamp that he developed in 1880 after his successful experimentation with filaments. This incandescent lamp was a valuable step in the development of electric lighting both for home and office. One of these lamps exists today in the William T. Hammer Collection of early lighting devices in New York.

Latimer's change in jobs was accompanied by changes at home. On June 12, 1883, he and Mary celebrated the birth of their first child, Emma Jeannette, after ten years of marriage. It was a loving home into which she was born. Her father found great comfort there; in fact, he spent much of his free time writing poems and painting pictures for his wife and little daughter.

Jeannette, as she preferred to be called, had big brown eyes and light brown skin. It was evident early on that she had inherited her father's talents in the arts. When she was young, Lewis would often entertain the family by playing his violin or flute. Jeannette composed the words and

The Latimers' first child, Emma Jeannette, was born in 1883. She grew up to be a musician.

music to short pieces and even sold her compositions to friends. Later, as a young woman, she studied at the Institute of Musical Art in New York and at Juilliard, a world-famous college of music. Piano was her specialty, and in her later life, she composed and taught music and performed in concert. A famous songwriter of the day, Harry T. Burleigh, even wrote a song for Jeannette that he entitled "Jean."

Jeannette's birth made 1883 a wonderful year for Lewis in his home life. But it was a year of defeat and frustration in the workplace. His new job did not last long. Soon after he went to work at Acme, that company, too, closed its doors. Seriously worried about being able to support his growing family, Lewis hurried to look for yet another job. He found it with Charles C. Perkins, head of the Imperial Electric Light Company. Perkins hired Latimer as a drafter and general assistant. Together, they went to Hartford, Connecticut, to work on a project with the Mather Electric Company.

The job at Imperial supported his family, but Latimer was dissatisfied and uneasy. He wanted to use his creative mind and his experience with inventing and drawing. He was no longer satisfied with being a drafter. In his dreams, he saw himself accomplishing greater things. What Latimer did not know was that during this time of frustration, he was being watched carefully by a man who would soon give him an opportunity to make his dreams happen.

CHAPTER SIX

ALONGSIDE
THOMAS ALVA
EDISON

Lewis Latimer worked especially hard from 1880, when Hiram Maxim hired him to work at the United States Electric Lighting Company, to 1884, by which time Latimer worked for the Imperial Electric Light Company. He had overcome great difficulty, continually needing to look for work to support himself and his family.

Nevertheless, during this time, Latimer filed a number of patents, experimented with and tested several inventions, and toyed with dozens of new ideas, some of which would eventually receive patents. What he really needed was an employer who appreciated his creative mind and gave him the freedom to explore more of his ideas. He found it in his association with one of the most productive inventors of the day, Thomas Alva Edison.

Working with "The Wizard"

During his lifetime, Edison was awarded 1,093 patents. The first one was for an electrical device to record votes in elections that he developed when he was just 22 years old. Seven years later, in 1876, he built the world's first private research and development laboratory in Menlo Park, New Jersey. It was here, in 1877, that he designed one of the inventions for which he is most famous: the phonograph. For this, Edison became known as "The Wizard of Menlo Park."

Just two years after inventing the phonograph, "The Wizard" received his patent on the incandescent lamp. The success of this invention drew the attention of several men with money. They saw promise in what Edison was doing and wanted to invest in the future of electricity. With the money they invested, the Edison Electric Light Company was born.

To promote his invention and make lighting available to a large number of people, Edison designed a lighting system for New York City's financial district. This system served as a model for other similar systems elsewhere. This model required that Edison create a variety of devices to make the system work: sockets, circuits, switches, junction boxes, relays, conduits, and more. To provide power for the station, he developed a large new dynamo, or generator. "In every direction stretched out long lines of electric lights, whose lustre made wide white circles on the white clad earth," wrote *The New York Herald*. "One could not tire of gazing at those starry lines."

Edison had earned his "Wizard" nickname honestly. He had the ability to solve seemingly unsolvable problems. But

In 1884, Thomas Edison hired Latimer to work at his
Electric Light Company offices in New York City.

while it was true that Edison was a wizard at invention, he was not a wizard at business. When it came to filing applications for his patents, providing the necessary detailed drawings, and keeping the complicated paperwork in order, Edison needed help. In fact, so poor was some of his record keeping that in 1883, the patent office ruled in favor of one of his rivals. It said that William Edward Sawyer had filed an application for an incandescent carbon-burning lamp before Edison had filed his. Edison had lost this particular race due to poor record keeping. He needed someone to help with this important aspect of the patent process.

The man Edison needed to help him with applications, drawings, and record keeping was Lewis Latimer. His qualifications for the job were excellent, and he had been in the lighting industry nearly since its beginning. He was also known as an extremely patient person who paid careful attention to details.

Just exactly when Latimer came to Edison's attention is unclear, but in 1884, he was approached by someone from the engineering department of the Edison Electric Light Company. Soon he was working as a drafter at the company in New York City. Eventually he would rise to the rank of chief drafter and patents expert in Edison's company.

LATIMER THE INVENTOR

At the time that he was hired, Latimer was experimenting on inventions of his own. On September 3, 1885, he filed for a patent on an "Apparatus for Cooling and Disinfecting." This was an early version of the room air conditioner. Not only was Latimer's device designed to cool a room, but it

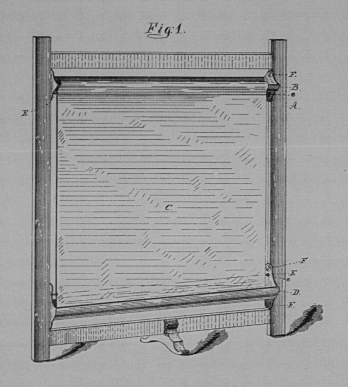

Lewis Latimer's 1886 patent was a type of early air conditioner. Mary Latimer's name appears as a witness.

could also be used to put purifying chemicals into the air. This feature could be valuable in hospitals or sickrooms where the air needed to be cleansed.

The invention consisted of a wooden frame, across which was stretched a large piece of wet cloth. There were two reservoirs on the top and bottom of the cloth that could hold water or the purifying chemicals. This frame was placed about a foot away from a window. As Latimer's patent application explains, "The warm air entering the apartment by the windows comes in contact with the moist surface of the webbing [cloth], evaporating the water therefrom, parting with some of its head in doing so, and creating a motion in the air of the room resulting in both cooling and changing [the air]."

The patent for the cooling device was approved on January 12, 1886. Like so many of Lewis Latimer's inventions, the cooling device was designed to make life easier, safer, and more pleasant for people.

On the drawing that accompanied the patent application, Mary W. Latimer's name appears as a witness. The patent office required that all inventors provide a drawing of their invention and that they sign the picture in the presence of two witnesses. By signing it, the inventors pledged that the idea originated with them and that they did not copy someone else's invention. The witnesses then signed their names, as proof of the inventor's claim.

Mary's acting as a witness was further proof of the Latimers' close relationship. Throughout their married life, she had shown a strong interest in her husband's career. Mary was one of Lewis's greatest supporters and gave him much encouragement, particularly when times were hard or he was out of work.

EDISON'S EXPERT WITNESS

Great changes were now happening in the field of electric lighting, and new equipment was being developed by dozens of different inventors. A great variety of new lighting companies sprang up, each one determined to become a giant in the field. Edison himself had started many companies, each independent of the others. The parent, or main, company was the Edison Electric Light Company of New York. In 1889, Edison's many companies joined to become Edison General Electric.

It was not uncommon at this time for inventors to sue one another over claims to patents or inventions. The courts were full of such cases. By 1890, the lawsuits had become so numerous and time-consuming that Edison General Electric formed a separate legal department, headed by William J. Jenks. Latimer was moved to this department. In his new position, he was sent to many parts of the country to gather information about Edison's inventions and other people's uses of them. This information was valuable when Edison's company was sued or when Edison found it necessary to sue other inventors who were trying to claim his ideas.

Latimer had many other responsibilities in his new job. He not only made technical drawings but was also expected to testify in court about Edison's inventions. He conducted research for Edison General Electric and looked over rival electrical plants.

One of Thomas Edison's most worrisome rivals was Hiram Maxim's United States Electrical Lighting Company. Knowing that Latimer had worked for Maxim for several years, Edison was interested in finding out some of the

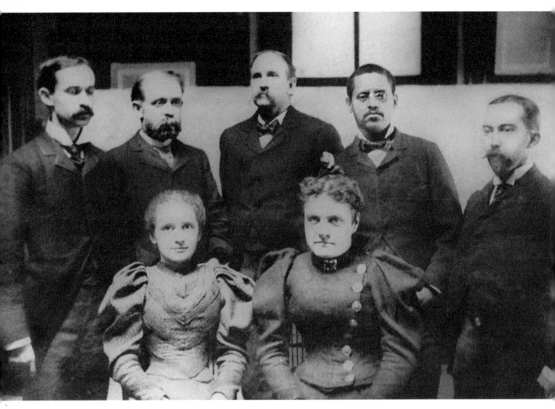

In 1890, Latimer (back row, second from right) moved to Edison General Electric's legal department. In this position, he often testified in court as an expert witness.

company's secrets. When two giants such as Edison and Maxim battled, a great deal of money was usually at stake. In fact, at this time, the two sides were locked in a legal battle over a patent on the incandescent lightbulb, which Maxim claimed to have invented before Edison. In 1886, a judge in St. Louis, Missouri, decided in Maxim's favor.

Upset over the Missouri judge's ruling, Edison filed an appeal, hoping to have the case heard by a higher court. During the hearings that followed, Latimer served as an expert witness for Edison. Because he was an expert in the field of electricity, the court relied on his statements to be absolutely accurate, down to the last detail. After much testimony, in which Latimer's knowledge was a tremendous help to his boss, the case was decided in Edison's favor.

Writing the Book on Electric Lighting

So new was the field of electric lighting that little had been written about it. In 1881, Edison's rival William Edward Sawyer had published a book on incandescent lighting. But since that time, there had been many changes and improvements in the industry. Edison's inventions and methods were now recognized as the best in the field. By 1890, Sawyer's book was badly in need of revision. Edison asked Latimer to revise the material and write a new, up-to-date book to replace Sawyer's.

Using both his technical knowledge and his talent for creative writing, Latimer compiled a book entitled *Incandescent Electric Lighting: A Practical Description of the Edison System*. In it, he praises Edison's greatest invention, the electric light: "Like the light of the sun, it beautifies all things on which it shines, and is no less welcome in the palace than in the humble home." Writing in a more technical style, Latimer explains the principle behind the incandescent lamp.

Latimer greatly respected Edison. And Edison, in turn, respected Latimer's knowledge of the field. He hoped that with Latimer's talent for writing, he could help the general public to understand this new and highly technical subject.

The result pleased Edison. Latimer presented the often dry, technical material in a way that the average person could understand. And in the book, he heaped great praise on the quality and reliability of the Edison system of electric lighting, as well as on Edison himself.

Incandescent Electric Lighting was short, only 140 pages long, and was illustrated with Latimer's own drawings. To make it longer, he asked two other men to contribute. Charles J. Fields wrote a piece called "Design and Operation of Incandescent Stations." John W. Howell, another electrical pioneer, did an article entitled, "The Maximum Efficiency of Incandescent Lamps."

Electrical engineers throughout the United States used the book as their standard reference, and it was sometimes called the "bible" of electric lighting. In one copy of the book, Latimer handwrote, "This was the first book on Electric Lighting published in the United States." Some historians believe that Latimer mistakenly thought that his book was the very first on the market. But it is more likely that he meant that the original Sawyer edition, updated with his own revisions, was truly the first.

By this time, Latimer had risen to the position of chief drafter in the Edison General Electric Company. He was also considered a patents expert and played a major role in the company's legal affairs. Now another major event happened in his life: a second daughter, Louise Rebecca, was born on April 19, 1890. Her first name was taken from her father; her middle name was her grandmother's.

Second daughter Louise Rebecca Latimer was born in 1890 and became a talented artist.

EDISON BOWS TO HIS RIVALS

One of the biggest conflicts facing Edison General Electric was Edison's insistence on using a direct current (DC) system of wiring. In electrical terms, current describes the movement of tiny particles called electrons through wires. Many of Edison's rivals preferred the alternating current (AC) system. With this type of wiring, the flow of electricity periodically reverses, or alternates, directions. In the DC system, which Edison preferred, the flow of electricity was always in the same direction.

Rivals said that AC systems could move electricity farther than DC, which was true. But AC was also more expensive and, Edison claimed, more dangerous.

One of Edison's rivals was a small company called Thomson-Houston. The other was Westinghouse, headed by inventor George Westinghouse. For three years, "The Wizard" watched his rivals get contracts for electrical systems in different cities, while his own attempts failed because he would not provide an AC system. As it turned out, his rivals were right: Alternating current proved to be the best system for bringing electricity into homes.

Edison's stubborn refusal to use AC cost his company a lot of money. The directors of Edison General Electric were upset. The best way to solve the problem, they decided, was to merge with one of the rivals that was becoming successful through the use of alternating current. So it was that, in 1892, Edison General Electric merged with its rival, the Thomson-Houston Company. The new firm was called the General Electric Company, which still exists today. Edison's name was dropped from the title, which angered him greatly. Disgusted and bitter, he ended any further involvement with General Electric except to defend his patents.

Lewis celebrated his second daughter's birth by painting a picture of her. This must have been a good omen for the child, because she grew up to become a talented artist in her own right. As a young woman, "Reba," as she liked to be called, attended college at Pratt Institute, a fine school for art and design in New York City. Eventually, she became a teacher in the public schools.

A Connection to His Father

Records do not show that either Reba or her older sister, Jeannette, ever met their grandfather. In fact, none of the family journals records that any of the Latimers ever again saw George, Sr.

But it appears that Lewis may have seen his father. On September 16, 1894, he received a letter from former slave and abolitionist Frederick Douglass. In it, Douglass referred to a letter that he had apparently received recently from Lewis, in which Lewis had mentioned George's poor health. Douglass was surprised to hear that George was ill, because Douglass had seen him during the previous spring, and George seemed well. Douglass also mentioned the excitement in Boston over George's capture more than half a century earlier.

John Wallace Hutchinson, one of the abolitionists who had helped George win his freedom, interviewed him in 1894. By this time, the former slave was 73. He walked with a cane and appeared to be partially paralyzed on one side. The interview was published in the appendix to a book that Hutchinson was writing. It quotes George as saying, "Forty-five years I pursued the trade of a paperhanger in Lynn."

Lynn was a town not far from Boston, and if George was working there all those years, then certainly he could have made contact with his family.

But even after all these years, he apparently had his reasons for staying away. Whatever they were, Lewis seemed to understand, for nothing he wrote expressed any resentment toward his father for having abandoned his family. Nor did George, Sr., mention his family or any reason for leaving them in his interview with Hutchinson.

DEALING WITH RACIAL ISSUES

It is clear from the letter about his father that, over the years, Lewis Latimer was in touch with Frederick Douglass. But Douglass was not the only well-known black leader with whom he had contact. He also corresponded with Booker T. Washington, a former slave who had become a teacher and founded the Tuskegee Institute in Alabama. Richard Greener, the first African American to graduate from Harvard University, also kept up a correspondence with Latimer. Greener was very active in the civil rights movement and urged Latimer to join the cause. "I am heart and soul into the movement," Latimer wrote back. " . . . it is our duty to show our country, and . . . the world that we are

Richard Greener worked for civil rights for African Americans.

Separate but Equal

Another event took place in 1896 that distressed all fair-minded people of Lewis Latimer's day. This was the Supreme Court's ruling in the case of *Plessy* v. *Ferguson*. This case involved Homer Adolph Plessy, a black man from Louisiana who was arrested for sitting in a railroad car reserved for white people. Plessy claimed that, because he was made to leave the white man's car, he was not being treated fairly. In the state court, Judge John H. Ferguson ruled against Plessy, saying that since the railroad had provided cars of equal quality for black people, Plessy's rights had not been violated. When the Supreme Court heard the case, it agreed. It held that "the Fourteenth Amendment of the U.S. Constitution guaranteed political but not social equality."

This was the beginning of the "separate but equal" battle that would rage in America for more than 50 years. It encouraged "legal segregation" in the South, where it was considered acceptable for blacks and whites to be separated in public places as long as the facilities (such as schools, train cars, and drinking fountains) were equal. And it was a huge step backward in the cause of civil rights.

looking to the interests of the country at large, when we protest against the crime and injustice meted out to any class or conditions of our citizens."

Latimer was not an outspoken radical, but he was a strong supporter of African-American rights. At one point, he wrote to Greener, "We should have a National Convention [of black Americans]. . . ." The convention would direct its energies, "to presenting . . . facts and figures showing . . . that ignorance and crime go hand in hand with prejudice; that schools and churches multiply where there is neither class nor color distinctions in the law. . . ."

In his many jobs, Latimer had never been the victim of outright hatred or gross discrimination. Still, he did not deny that race had been a barrier for him. He mentioned this in his journal, when writing about his years in the engineering department at Edison General Electric. New workers tried to pretend, said Latimer, that he could not do as good a job as they. But his tremendous skill could not be ignored. Latimer believed that education and achievement were two of the keys to breaking down the racial barrier. Latimer himself was living proof of this point, for he continued to distinguish himself in his field.

THE BOARD OF PATENT CONTROL IS BORN

On March 24, 1896, Latimer applied for yet another patent, this one for "Locking Rack for Hats, Coats, Umbrellas." This useful invention offered people a more secure system for checking their hats and coats in restaurants or hotel lobbies. Until this time, customers hung their coats or hats in a coatroom while they ate or conducted business, hoping that their belongings would be safe. But Latimer's device provided a lock on the rack that allowed only the customer to retrieve his or her belongings. Latimer described his invention as "simple, efficient, and inexpensive. . . ." He claimed that it would "occupy very little space and . . . can be readily secured in position." Even today, some large hotels and other establishments still use this Latimer creation.

In May 1896, George Latimer, Sr., died in Lynn, Massachusetts. No mention of his death is made in Lewis's journals. That same year, Latimer was appointed to the new Board of Patent Control, made up of representatives from

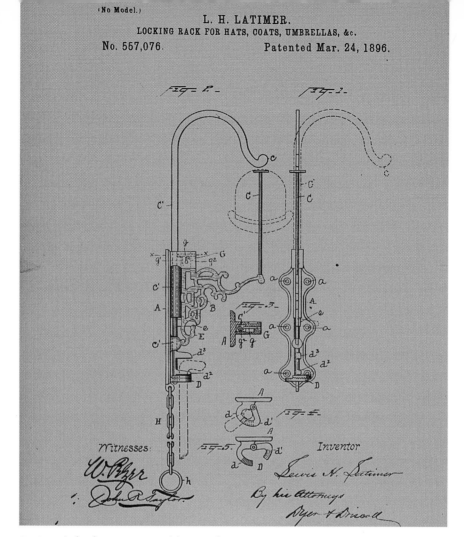

(No Model.)

L. H. LATIMER.

LOCKING RACK FOR HATS, COATS, UMBRELLAS, &c.

No. 557,076.   Patented Mar. 24, 1896.

Latimer's locking coat and hat rack invention is
still used today in some hotels and restaurants.

the General Electric Company and its rival, Westinghouse.
By forming the board, they hoped to cut down on the number of lawsuits, both between themselves and with other
companies or inventors. Such suits were time-consuming
and costly. Latimer's boss from the legal department at
Edison General Electric, William Jenks, directed the board.
Latimer himself acted as head drafter and as expert witness,
positions for which he was well qualified. He served on the
board for 15 years as one of its most valuable members.

CHAPTER SEVEN

"A MODEL FOR TODAY'S YOUTH"

Dignified, competent, friendly—that is how people who worked with Lewis Latimer often described him. Throughout his long career, Latimer was considered to be an extremely talented and reliable professional. He was highly respected by his coworkers.

He always got along well with his white coworkers, but Latimer made sure that he did so without "losing touch with his roots." He maintained a strong pride in his African-American heritage and worked to improve daily life for black people.

A Quiet Spokesman for Equality

While Latimer did not expect society to give African Americans special treatment, he did try, in his firm, quiet way, to ensure that blacks received fair treatment. For example, when S. R. Scottron, the only black member of the Brooklyn School Board, was not reappointed to another term, Latimer took action. He wrote a letter to Seth Low, the mayor of New York City, pointing out that the mayor's job was to represent all the people—of all racial groups and nationalities—of the city. He went on to urge the mayor to reappoint Scottron, not simply because he was a black but also because he was a good citizen and a good representative for all the people of the city. Unfortunately, the letter drew little notice, and Scottron was not reappointed to the board.

But that did not discourage Latimer. He was committed to the cause of civil rights at a time when the movement was in its infancy. In a paper he wrote on racial equality, Latimer argued that it was necessary for African Americans to show that they had proven themselves, despite innumerable barriers, to be worthy citizens of the United States.

Pride in Country and Community

Latimer never forgot his humble beginnings. Throughout his life, he helped others who were trying to improve their own lives. Soon after the turn of the century, his concern brought him to the Henry Street Settlement. This center provided job training, health care, and other services for immigrants who had recently arrived in New York City. Few of the immigrants were black; most were Jews from Russia and Eastern Europe. They were poor, as Latimer once had been. They had few job skills and no knowledge of English.

When the Henry Street Settlement asked Latimer to help, he volunteered eagerly. It had long been his belief that, by improving ourselves in the present, we improve our future. At night after work, he taught English to the immigrants. For those who were interested, he offered a course in technical drawing, which he had taught himself so long ago with his used books and secondhand drafting tools.

Many years after Latimer's death, the Henry Street Settlement presented his granddaughter, Winifred Latimer Norman, Jeannette's daughter, with a tribute in honor of his countless hours of help:

The self-educated son of a run-away slave, whose brilliant achievements and creative spirit led to the development of the light bulb, the telephone, and the Age of Electricity. A man of international fame and honor, who shared his talents with the Henry Street Settlement. In recognition of the time and knowledge he so generously gave us.

Latimer was a patriotic person as well. For many years, he was a proud member of the Grand Army of the Republic (GAR). This was an organization of Union Civil War veterans who worked to keep alive the memory of that war and to teach schoolchildren about it. The GAR also worked with the government to see that pensions were paid to veterans. Photographs show Latimer standing proudly in his GAR uniform during the time he served as a staff officer.

In his community of Flushing, in the Queens borough of New York, Latimer headed a group planning to establish a Unitarian church. Unitarians believe in being tolerant—that

In 1915, Latimer (left, holding flag) posed with other members of the Grand Army of the Republic.

is, in accepting other people's backgrounds and points of view. They do not have one set of ideas or beliefs on which all members must agree. Instead, they study a wide variety of religions. Latimer practiced tolerance in all aspects of his life, so it is natural that he would be drawn to this type of religion.

The church was completed in 1908, and it remains a strong force in the community today. Latimer's grand-daughter, Winifred Latimer Norman, has been active in the

Lewis Latimer

local church and has served for years on the national and international Unitarian staff as well.

In his professional life, Latimer continued his work with the Board of Patent Control. During that time, he suffered from increasing problems with his vision. The fine, detailed drawing work that he had done all his life was beginning to take its toll. Still, he continued to work on inventions, do technical drawings, and prepare patent applications.

"A Model for Today's Youth"

Latimer continued to work into his sixties.

Lewis Latimer

Although he did not work on inventions with such dedication as he had in earlier days, he still had patents pending on several new ideas. One was a system of book supports, designed to keep books from falling or getting bent when they were lined up on a shelf. In his patent applications, Latimer pointed out that the support could be "cut and pressed from a single piece of sheet metal, so that it has the advantage of being easily constructed and involving small expense." Being a lover and collector of books, he may well have designed the supports to meet his own needs.

A LIFETIME OF ACCOMPLISHMENT

As he aged, Latimer's eyesight continued to diminish. Even though he had been on the forefront of the age of electricity, lighting conditions in most offices were a long way from perfect. Most lamps did not provide light that was strong enough for working long hours at the close, detailed work such as he had done. Although he never went blind, it became increasingly difficult for Latimer to do the type of work he knew best.

In 1911, Lewis and Mary's daughter Jeannette was married. Her husband, Gerald Norman, was a high school teacher who had grown up on the Caribbean island of Jamaica. The couple had two children. Their son, Gerald Norman, Jr., served as an administrative law judge, and their daughter, Winifred Latimer Norman, devoted her life to social work. Both of them spent much of their adult lives preserving their grandfather's name and his accomplishments.

Also in 1911, the Board of Patent Control was abolished, and Latimer was once again out of work. It could have been

"A Model for Today's Youth"

In this drawing, entitled *My Situation as It Looked to Me in 1912*, Latimer takes a humorous look at his predicament after he lost his job.

very difficult for a man of 63 to find employment, but Latimer was fortunate. The board's chief technical assistant, Edwin Hammer, was an engineer and patent lawyer who had his own private firm, Hammer & Schwarz. He knew Latimer's work well and admired what he had done for the Board of Patent Control. Hammer invited Latimer to join his firm, an offer that the inventor accepted gladly. For the next 13 years, he served as a patent consultant for Hammer.

During this time, Edwin's brother William T. Hammer was compiling a history of the Edison organization. Part of that history was a huge collection of lamps. Eventually, he gathered some 800 lamps; today, they are preserved in the William T. Hammer Collection in New York City. Among them is the Latimer lamp.

In the mid-1970s, the prestigious Henry Ford Museum in Dearborn, Michigan, sponsored a special exhibit featuring Latimer's contributions to electric lighting. During this exhibit, the nearly 100-year-old Latimer lamp from the Hammer collection was lit—after much testing to be sure it would not be harmed in any way. It had been nearly a century since this great invention had been created, but the lamp still burned with the same brightness and reliability that it had in Latimer's day!

Another of William Hammer's efforts as electric lighting historian was to gather those men who had been pioneers in the field for a reunion on Thomas Alva Edison's seventy-first birthday, February 11, 1918. The group was made up of people who had worked with Edison prior to 1885, and Lewis Latimer was among the chosen 28. Every year after that, the Edison Pioneers met, and Latimer was always in attendance. To be a member of the Edison Pioneers was the highest honor that one could receive in the electric lighting industry.

Latimer (front row, second from left) stands proudly with the other members of the Edison Pioneers in 1920.

Latimer received a diploma from the Edison Pioneers during the 1921 meeting. It described the group in this way:

An association formed to bring together in friendly intercourse the men who have been associated with Mr. Thomas

Alva Edison and his interests in the United States of America or abroad. Who desire to pay tribute to his transcendent genius, to bear testimony to his achievements, to acknowledge the affection and esteem in which they hold him, and as far as lies within their power to do good deeds in his name.

"A Model for Today's Youth"

Lewis Latimer did his part to "bear testimony" to Edison's achievements in a poem he composed for one of the meetings. It is entitled "Tom Edison":

> Who caught the lightning from the skies
> And bade it gladden human eyes
> To fill the whole world with surprise
> > Tom Edison
>
> Who made the night vie with the day
> Who bade the darkness speed away
> As willed the world to work or play
> > Tom Edison
>
> If there be those who took their part
> To aid him in his work and art
> They'r glad they lent both head and heart
> > Tom Edison
>
> His race is very nearly run
> But this great land has since begun
> To know the worth of this her son
> > Tom Edison

During his lifetime, many of Latimer's poems were published in magazines and newspapers. Sometimes he received a small payment for them, but more often he did not. Of greater importance to Lewis Latimer was the appreciation that others had for his writings—his prose, plays, and poetry. He was a man who had a great deal to say on many important topics, and these works allowed him to express himself.

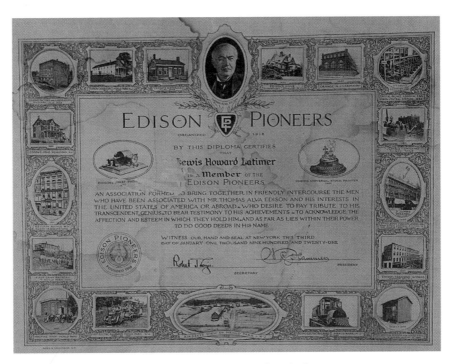

In 1921, the Edison Pioneers gave Latimer this diploma, which certified his membership in the group.

Old Age Takes Its Toll

One year before Lewis retired from Hammer's firm, he and Mary celebrated their fiftieth wedding anniversary. It was a splendid occasion. Their two grandchildren and dozens of other relatives and friends came from near and far.

This time, however, the literary praise was written not *by* Latimer but *for* him. The praise came in the form of a letter written by Elmer Schwarz, Edwin Hammer's partner, and it was dedicated to Lewis and Mary. All of the employees at the company of Hammer & Schwarz signed the letter, which read:

It speaks for both of you that each has put up with the other for so long a time; this statement is directed especially to Mr. Latimer, whose idiosyncrasies [strange habits] we know so well. But we find that during the forty years of his connection with electrical matters he does not appear to have made any but friends of those with whom he has been associated . . . .

As Mary and Lewis became older, they were fortunate to have their daughter Reba move in with and care for them. Jeannette and her family lived near the Latimer home on Holly Avenue in Flushing, Queens. And it was here, less than a year after their grand fiftieth anniversary celebration, that Mary Wilson Latimer died.

Lewis had his wife's body taken back to her hometown of Fall River, Massachusetts. Mary was buried there in the Oakwood Cemetery.

Without his wife of 50 years, and with his own health failing, the old inventor went into a state of depression. In just a short time, a stroke paralyzed him on one side.

In an effort to cheer up their father, Reba and Jeannette put together a book of his poetry. Although some of his poems had been published in magazines or newspapers over the years, they had never been collected together into a book. For his seventy-seventh birthday, on September 4, 1925, his daughters presented him with 50 copies of the collection, entitled *Poems of Love and Life*. The book, which was printed on handmade Italian paper, was illustrated with photos of Lewis's wife and children.

Half of the poems were about life, and half were about love. Among the love poems was "Ebon Venus," the one that he had written for Mary shortly before their wedding. One of the poems about life was titled "Friends":

Friend of my childhood,
Of life's early days
When together we wandered
Through bright sunny ways
Each true to the other,
Till full manhood came,
And found the old friendship
As ever the same.

Came summer and winter,
Years waxed and waned.
Youth it had left us
But friendship remained
And now as with white locks
I bend o'er life's page
The friend of my childhood
Is the friend of my age.

PART OF A GREAT TEAM

Lewis Latimer lived another three years before finally succumbing to poor health on December 11, 1928. Among the many tributes to Latimer that were written in newspapers at the time of his death was this one, in the December 19 issue of the *Amsterdam News:* "His work in science was an achievement and his personal life was a work of art."

The Edison Pioneers also wrote a tribute in memory of their only African-American member. It was entered into the organization's permanent records by William H. Meadowcroft, historian for the group, who was for many years Thomas Alva Edison's private secretary. It read:

Lewis Howard Latimer was one of the colored race . . . and was one of those to respond to the initial call that led to the formation of the Edison Pioneers, January 24th, 1918. Broad-mindedness, versatility in the accomplishment of things intellectual and cultural, a linguist, a devoted husband and father, all were characteristic of him, and his genial presence will be missed from our gatherings. . . . We hardly mourn his inevitable going so much as we rejoice in pleasant memory of having been associated with him in a great work for all peoples under a great man [Edison].

The tribute ended with this statement: "Mr. Latimer was a full member and an esteemed one, of the Edison Pioneers." This was the honor that Lewis Latimer considered the greatest of his life. He was proud to have been a member of such a respected group. Like most inventors, he realized that progress in technology can never be credited to one person alone. Invention is an ongoing team effort. Inventors learn from one another, build on one another's ideas, and carry on the work of those who have come before them. All the credit for developing the carbon lamp filament cannot go to Lewis Latimer or any other single inventor. In developing his filament, he changed and improved upon the ideas of other people who were also experimenting with the process. These included Thomas Edison and Hiram Maxim in the United States, Sir Joseph Wilson Swan and Frederick de Moleyns in England, Alexandre de Lodyguine in Russia, and a number of other inventors around the world. Many of Lewis Latimer's patents, like those of most other inventors, were improvements on existing devices. It is in this "building block" way that new technology is developed in our world.

Mary and Lewis Latimer stand with their
daughter Reba on the porch of their home.

Latimer's Legacy Lives On

For a man who had been born to runaway slaves, abandoned by his father, and raised in poverty by a single mother, Lewis Latimer had accomplished a miracle. Despite his lack of formal schooling, he had educated himself. Despite the fact that blacks were largely scorned and shunned in his day, he made a place for himself in a white world. His own sense of self-respect earned him the respect of scientists, inventors, businesspeople, and professionals around the world. He did not blame his parents for his disrupted childhood, nor society for its treatment of blacks. Instead, he directed his energy toward overcoming these obstacles. Quietly he forged ahead, determined to carve for himself a life of achievement and accomplishment.

The legacy that Lewis Latimer left the world is remembered today at many fine museums and institutions. In the 1970s, the Henry Ford Museum in Dearborn, Michigan, sponsored a special exhibit devoted to Latimer's work. He was among those honored in a traveling exhibit entitled "Black Scientists and Inventors," arranged by the Museum of Science and Industry in Chicago, Illinois, in the mid-1970s. During Black History Month in 1984, the Edison National Historic Site in New Jersey held a special tribute to Latimer in which his grandchildren took part. And for seven months during 1995, the Queens Borough Public Library in New York presented an exhibit on Lewis Latimer's life entitled "Blueprint for Change."

His grandchildren, as well as the descendants of his sister, Margaret Hawley, have worked tirelessly to preserve Latimer's name and memory. They acted as advisers on a

Throughout his life, Latimer's family was a great source of happiness. This 1923 portrait was taken before Mary (front row, center) died.

filmstrip that was made on the inventor's life. They cooperated with the Queens Historical Society in Flushing, New York, and with the Queens Borough Public Library to preserve his papers, books, drawings, and other artifacts.

In 1988, they helped organize a drive to save the Latimer house in Flushing, which was scheduled to be torn down to make room for a new housing development. The group's goal was to raise $36,000 to move the house about a mile from its Holly Avenue location. The new home would be in a field across from the Latimer Gardens Public Housing

Project, also named for the inventor. Through hard work, funds were raised in time to save the house from destruction. Today it is being restored, with plans to open a museum in the house devoted to Latimer's life and achievements.

Lewis Latimer managed to score great accomplishments at a time when it was very difficult for people from poor, black families to achieve any kind of equal standing. A major factor in his success was his positive outlook on the world. He firmly believed that life was filled with opportunities if a person had the determination and willingness to work hard to take advantage of them.

Forty-five years after Lewis Howard Latimer's death, the Thomas Alva Edison Foundation, the General Electric Company, and the Henry Ford Museum issued a booklet outlining his life and accomplishments. The booklet called Latimer "a model for today's youth" and reminded all of us that we live better because of what he and his associates contributed to the modern world. "This outstanding man had the courage to dream an ambitious dream and make it come true. His accomplishments, although little known, prove that a determined person can make good no matter what the odds are against him or her."

GLOSSARY

abolitionist A person who favored abolishing, or doing away with, slavery.

alternating current (*AC*) Electric current that periodically changes or alternates the direction in which it flows.

apprentice A person who is bound to work for a certain period of time with someone more experienced and from whom he or she will learn a skill or trade in exchange for the hours of work.

arc light Light produced when a flow of electric current jumps across a break or arc between pieces of carbon connected to two wires.

carbonize To turn a material into carbon by a process such as heating.

cellulose One of the chemical substances that make up wood, paper, or cardboard.

circuit In electricity, the path taken by an electric current.

Confederacy The government formed when 11 southern states seceded from (withdrew from) the Union just before the Civil War. Those states were Alabama, Arkansas, Florida, Georgia, Louisiana, Mississippi, North Carolina, South Carolina, Tennessee, Texas, and Virginia.

current The flow of electricity through wires or other conductors. This current is measured both by the amount of electricity that is flowing and by the rate at which it flows.

direct current (*DC*) Electric current that always flows in the same direction.

drafter A person who makes technical drawings, plans, or sketches, often for engineering projects; also draftsman.

dynamo A machine that converts mechanical power into electrical power.

electron A tiny particle of negatively charged electrical energy. Together with protons and neutrons, electrons make up atoms, the main ingredient of all matter.

emancipation Freedom from bondage or slavery.

filament A thin, threadlike conductor of electricity found inside a lightbulb that heats to produce light when an electric current is passed through it.

fugitive One who flees or tries to escape.

incandescence A glowing, white light produced in a bulb when the filament is heated to a high temperature by electric current passing through it.

parallel wiring A system of wiring in which a series of lights is connected to one source and each light gets the full amount of electricity that the source can provide. When one light burns out, the others continue to burn. It is the opposite of series wiring.

patent A guarantee from the government (through the U.S. Patent Office) to an inventor that he or she is the only one who may allow that product to be made or sold.

pending Awaiting, not yet decided.

petition A formal or legal request for a group or organization to take certain action.

platinum A heavy, precious-metal element that has a high melting point and is a conductor of electricity.

reservoir A place where a liquid is stored.

resistance In electronics, an object or a force that makes it difficult for the current to pass along its circuit.

segregation The separating or setting apart of one racial group from another.

series wiring A system of wiring in which a series of

lights is connected to one source and each light gets only a portion of electricity that the source provides. When one light burns out, the whole series fails. It is the opposite of parallel wiring.

testimony A statement made under oath, usually in a court of law.

tolerance A willingness to respect or understand other people's habits or beliefs.

transmit To send, pass, or cause to move from one place to another, such as an electrical current along a wire.

Underground Railroad The secret system used in the years before the Civil War for moving slaves from the southern states to the northern states and often into Canada, where they would be free. It was not an actual railroad.

Union The United States of America.

vacuum A completely empty space, where no matter exists—not even air.

FURTHER READING

Brodie, James Michael. *Created Equal: The Lives and Ideas of Black American Innovators.* New York: William Morrow and Company, 1993.

Coil, Suzanne M. *The Civil Rights Movement.* New York: Twenty-First Century Books, 1995.

Green, Carol. *Thomas Alva Edison, Bringer of Light.* Chicago: Children's Press, 1985.

Haber, Louis. *Black Pioneers of Science and Invention.* New York: Harcourt, Brace & World, Inc., 1970.

Hayden, Robert C. *Eight Black American Inventors.* Reading, MA: Addison-Wesley, 1972.

————. *Nine African American Inventors*. New York: Twenty-First Century Books, 1992.

Norman, Winifred Latimer, and Lily Patterson. *Lewis Latimer*. New York: Chelsea House Publishers, 1994.

Parker, Steve. *Thomas Edison & Electricity*. New York: HarperCollins, 1992.

Pollard, Michael. *The Lightbulb and How It Changed the World*. New York: Facts On File, 1995.

Turner, Glennette Tilley. *Lewis Howard Latimer*. Englewood Cliffs, NJ: Silver Burdett Press, 1991.

SOURCES

Baldwin, Neil. *Edison: Inventing the Century*. New York: Hyperion, 1995.

Brodie, James Michael. *Created Equal: The Lives and Ideas of Black American Innovators*. New York: William Morrow and Company, 1993.

Conot, Robert. *A Streak of Luck: The Life & Legend of Thomas Alva Edison*. New York: Seaview Books, 1979.

"Edison's Inventions" (pamphlet). West Orange, NJ: Edison National Historic Site, 1994.

Fried, Joseph P. "A Campaign to Remember an Inventor." *The New York Times*, August 6, 1988.

Green, Carol. *Thomas Alva Edison, Bringer of Light*. Chicago: Children's Press, 1985.

Haber, Louis. *Black Pioneers of Science and Invention*. New York: Harcourt, Brace & World, Inc., 1970.

Hayden, Robert C. *Eight Black American Inventors*. Reading, MA: Addison-Wesley, 1972.

Koolakian, Robert G. *Thomas Alva Edison's Associate: Lewis*

Howard Latimer. Dearborn, MI: Thomas Alva Edison
Foundation, Inc., 1973.

Norman, Winifred Latimer, and Lily Patterson. *Lewis
Latimer.* New York: Chelsea House Publishers, 1994.

Schneider, Janet M., and Bayla Singer, eds. *Blueprint for
Change: The Life and Times of Lewis H. Latimer.* Jamaica,
NY: Queens Borough Public Library, 1995.

Smith, Duane E., ed. *We the People: The Citizen and the Constitution.* Calabasas, CA: Center for Civic Education, 1995.

Turner, Glennette Tilley. *Lewis Howard Latimer.* Englewood
Cliffs, NJ: Silver Burdett Press, 1991.

Whittier, John Greenleaf. *The Poetical Works of Whittier.*
Boston: Houghton Mifflin Co., 1975.

Yanak, Ted, and Pam Cornelison. *The Great American
History Fact-Finder.* Boston: Houghton Mifflin, 1993.

INDEX

Boldfaced, italicized page numbers include picture references.

Lewis Latimer

Olmstead, Margaret, 11

Patents, 8, 38, 39, 60, 74, 75. *See also* Board of Patent Control
Perkins, Charles C., 68
Plessy, Homer Adolph, 82
Poems of Love and Life, 98

Sawyer, William Edward, 72, 77
Sayer, Mary D., 16–17
Schwarz, Elmer, 97
Scott, Dred, 28–*29*
Scottron, S. R., 86
segregation, 82
Sewall, Samuel E., 18, 22
Shaw, Lemuel, 22
Sherman, William Tecumseh, 36
slavery
  in America, 24–26, 28. *See also* Civil War
  end of, 36
  Massachusetts' petition to end, 23–26
  people who opposed. *See* abolitionists
slaves
  auctions for, *25*
  civil rights of former, 37, 39. *See also* civil rights movement

freedom for, 34
married, 12, 17
returned to Africa, 25
runaway, 14, 16. *See also* Douglass, Frederick; Latimer, George

Telephone, invention of, 45–47
Thirteenth Amendment, 36
Thomson-Houston electric company, 79
Tregoning, John, 57, 59

Underground Railroad, 14
United States. *See also* Civil War
  after Civil War, 37
  immigrants in, 86–87
  slavery in, 24–26, 28
U.S. Electric Lighting Company, 52, 55, 57, 59–61, 66, 75–76

Washington, Booker T., 81
Washington, George, 24
Watson, Thomas, 46
Westinghouse, George, electric company of, 79, 84
Weston, Edward, 63
Whittier, John Greenleaf, 20, *21*
Wright, Isaac, 32